attention

by poor here is mentioned person who has lack in all areas of life (material, emotional, even in relationships). But since so many painful truths will be told, someone will inavitably become heartbroken.

So, Poor – is not offense! - And if someone is insulted by the truth, it's not my problem.

Contents

it is impossible not to repeat the topics that I have not mentioned before in other books, papers, articles, courses, or even in daily posts. Because all my work is based on the principle of creating strong, successful and realized people. Therefore, in all my works, I have touched on the ways to escape, defeat and swallow the weaknesses inside us. Starting with envy, continuing with poverty, or getting rid of traitors. However, this work, unlike the others, will only deal with the topic of poverty, and if I have to take the same knowledge, from some other books, I will finally add, expand and improve the part that I have created so far.

To understand who is talking about all this, will tell you that I am person who became best-selling author at the age of 23 and my book was in a first place of selling lists for 7 month in a row in my own country. At the age of 25 or 26, I became speaker at international business forum UNIQ and was standing in one stage with Nick vujicic, I am three bestsellers author and am just 27 years old. if that information gives you anything, I have already bought my dream car, my fridge is always full by food, I'm not struggling financially, but I'm not rich either.

I'm not in the top 1% of humanity, but when it comes to creating the right environment, having decent and strong people around me, and fulfilling my dreams and desires, I'm already successful at that.

Also I am co-author of a book that will be published soon, written by world-renowned people such as John Maxwell (author of several world bestsellers), Nick Vujicic, and others.

However, these victories do not mean that many of the characteristics that has poor people (whether material, spiritual, or physical) do not characterize me. on the contrary, I personally have these qualities, and to tell you frankly, they are part of my daily struggle, because **the more I overcome "poverty" factors in myself, the more prosperity is comming into my life,** and the main reason why this book is being written now is , to discover new "points of weakneses" in myself, to after overcome them and enter a higher level of well-being.

Let's start with the fact that about half year ago, I conducted an internal survey among my customers who were taking self-confidence course from me (it was more than 1000 people) and the purpose of the survey was to get to know better the people who trusted me, were ready to work with me as an psychologist. In addition, a few days before the survey, I heard such an ideal saying, which was: "Our customers - are not us, and first of all, only for whom we are a role model are byuing our info products from us" and therefore, I wondered who are the people who wanted to live like me?

The survey consisted of 11 important questions, but most importent was: "What is the most unsatisfied problem for you?", the answers to which were so similar that it was impossible not to pay attention, and it consisted around the words "lack of money!"...

Most of the people wrote a word that was not relevant to me at that moment, that I had not been worried about for a long time, and if my current problems were how to buy an apartment, increase income from 10,000 to 20,000 Dollars, how to make my car beautiful, which new business should I start And so over and over again, people talled me that they are nowhere near the situation I am in, and so, because of it, I created a psychology of money online course aimed at improving the financial situation of my customers.

There I taught everything that I knew, considered, and in the end I even saw that it turns out that not others, but me personally, made a lot of mistakes in life, as a result of which I was in the state I was in and not a single step higher. I eventually got to the point where I teach people about wellness, but in reality - it turns out that me personally is making many of the same mistakes that they do. (It turns out that I am heading towards an inevitable defeat when my I become just tired)... In short, I had a lot of things to correct, which in the future led to the fact that I personally began to translate my own books into English language and export them abroad (ike any poor person: I was waiting for the perfect moment - perfect translator, time, the arrangement of opportunities, and I did nothing to make my main dream come true).

- If you don't know, my main dream is to become the author of world bestseller books, but I am the author of only 3 bestseller books in Georgia (which is nothing to worldwide). - Believe me, for really successful people, the work I do and the numbers I earn are too small. Acordingly to this situation, this book is created...

First of all, I have main questions:

- What brought me to the point that I am successful person, but don't have real success?

- Why is it that the majority of influencers in the world are poor (believe me, I know a lot of people who have hundreds of thousands of subscribers, recognition, shows and applause in their lives), but none of them can make as much money as you can imagine.

(To give a simple example, I met one of the well-known faces who had his own branded product at home, the existence of which I knew nothing about, and I liked the idea so much that imagined he could make at least 50,000 $ with this product per month, if this product is being advertised well... I ask, did the product sell well? And he says yes, I said how much and 50 pieces (we are talking about a profit of 500 $, no more)) - My God, I earned a hundred times more by selling the book, I thought.

The second simple example is that the majority of influencers, Youtubers, Tiktokers, writers, singers, sportsmen and people who are apparently successful in this business are actually poor and all they get in exchange for their energy is people's praise, recognition, etc. And being invited to other shows and even getting a lot of hate when they do something loud, ill-considered.

So, where does the psychology of real poverty

come from?

- This is what we will talk about in this work.

- Collective irresponsibility.
Let's start with the fact that poverty is diverse and many things, poor people, in different countries, have been formed in different ways, and although many features unite them, but **we must always remember that poverty is diverse!**

Accordingly, some traits are often repeated in society, while others, as it is already clear to smart person, rarely (if I will talk about individual traits somewhere, I will tell you that it is so, if I tell you about something that unites the majority, the same will be here).

So, What unites poor people in all countries is a collective irresponsibility, when people believe nothing depends on them, but this does not mean that such people do not want a good life. Therefore, unlike a responsible person, poor are generally looking for a savior and problem solver already from outside (instead of themselves).

For example, the reason for Argentina's current economic collapse is collective irresponsibility, when people year after year believe that someone special will come and solve all existing and current problems, but:

1. No one on earth can solve everyone's problems and

2. No one on earth can fully satisfy person who blames their responsibility on someone else.

With these words, I want to say that poverty first of all comes from relying on others, that your father, or mother, grandmother, or even the president will save you, but you yourself - believe that nothing depends on you, that you cannot change life, and therefore, this type of poor People are too bad in satisfying their own needs first.

- What do I mean by these words?

- I mean that any human, like any animal, has specific needs. which at any stage of life moves and motivates us to do or not do something. Whether we like it or not, these needs must be satisfyied, and experienced psychologists can easily see how well person knows how to satisfy his own needs, or does not knows. For example, in my online course of „psychology of relashionships" from the first lesson to the end, I teach participants such an important truth as the following: that it does not matter what our partner is like, **What matters is who we are, and if we are so good (as we think about ourselves), bad people will not stand beside us.** Therefore, expecting your partner to treat you better and only then giving him what he needs is irresponsible behavior and shows that you are not taking responsibility for being an adult in the relationship by yourself, but choosing position for someone else to do the work.

I understand that it is little unclear at first, but now you will understand what I am saying: the majority of people see the basis for fixing any kind of relationship in others (that the partner should change, appreciate us, not treat us badly, mother or father should pay more attention to us and so on endlessly – but at this time, we don't need to change our actions and ourselves, because we are too perfects), but not one of them, even for a second, considers and does not accept as true that „**if I am a strong and respectable person, no one will treat me badly and if someone tries, I will punish this person too Strictly, that's why, I am respectable person (because I know, how to defend myself)**". - A simple example to prove these words would be how the majority of people behave when they meet an envious person?

- They try to appease envy one. Give gifts, transfer money, solve their problems, and when this envy gets stronger, they blame the envious - but they don't even say who in reality is stupid here, that they didn't have enough courage to put person in his place at the first moment of disrespect (or even say: Who do you think you are, or who gave you the right to treat me like this? or even: don't treat me badly anymore) or throw this person out of their existence no matter what.

In short, here is question, why fool one helps to envious person?

(Because he doesn't want to feel guilty, make excuses (which the jealous person sometimes forces), he doesn't want to be scolded, get bad reputation, and therefore, he does what the parasitic personality asks of him, and finally: fool one is giving to envy the right to give first one internal satisfaction of the need for peace.

(I mean, fool is giving a right and instrument to envy: that second can make decision, does first one deserve being calm, or deserve to feel guilty?)

In short, he does not start to calm himself, but waits for the fact that envious person will someday change, correct, improve his actions and stop making him feel guilty **(but your honor is your own responsibility and they don't know that).**

the same is in relationships: when I posted video, in wich I was speaking „look at your partner with bright eyes, because it is a way to give your partner love", women wrote comments that they will do it, only after men deserve it.

- It turns out that what? (you will ask).

- Here too, person waits for someone to change and only after they will start giving love to their partners... but it is irresponsible in every ways...

It is irresponsible to yourself, that you are living with person, who does not diserve your bright eyes.

It is irresponsible to nature rules, that are telling us, that in a natural way, we have bright eyes (that is excitement) only after the moment of acquaintance, from 3 minutes to 3 years. (That means: there will inevitably come moment when, no matter what your partner does, you will no longer be able to admire him, or her as a best man or woman, and therefore it depends on you and only you, how can you manually make yourself start admiring your partner and telling him, or her, how gratfull you are, because of their existence).

But in reality, here too, person waits for someone else to change, but himself does nothing, except for repeating the same mistakes made before, which about they think are making them good person. (it's like in childhood, we are killing our partner with attention, and when they run away from us (because too much attention is making person unhappy), we think that they could not see good in us, but will not ever admit, that our attention comes not from that we are good partners, but from our fears, much time that is not used in good ways and other problems)...

And in money and material well-being, exactly the same thing happens. **Most of the people are doomed to poverty because they are willing to pass the responsibility on to others.** Expect someone else to change, save, help, but this is impossible! Just as I thought that perfect publishing house would appear abroad and notice my results, after wich they will publish my books and make me multi-millionaire, it is exactly the same here. (Not a single publishing house appeared in my life. No one was interested in my books, despite the fact that they are the best sellers in our country, and no one even answered to me on my emails), because of what I myself started translating and editing my books, no matter how good they will be translated, or even edited – first of all is to take responsibily to only try changing something.

It is the same with any kind of poverty.

Any idea that is built on the good wishes

of others and receiving prosperity as a result, is the cause of poverty and nothing else, which forces you to live in the same problems from day to day, and in short, the solution is actually to learn to satisfy yourself.

- What do I mean here?

- I mean that in relationship course, I have one lesson in which I teach and show people what needs we have as humans, what our partner expects subconsciously and how to satisfy those needs of our partners. In this lesson I share the following truth:

Both men and women have their own basic needs in relationships.

man expects recognition, teamwork, loyalty, sex and that he will give something (especially materially).

And a woman expects security, care, attention and appreciation. also sex and that she will get something in relationships.

All this is interconnected.

For example, recognition (it is when you look at your man with bright eyes, praise him, when you give compliments, cook some dishes, or even change your last to his, or do not interfere with choosing a name for child), but it becomes impossible to give this actions when man does not gives you to feel safe - When he beats you, fights with you, oppresses, belittles you, criticizes, or even doesn't earn money and doesn't even try to earn it... at this time you can't look at a person with bright eyes and subconsciously, because of it, he takes away your sense of security. Because of what, the relationship falls in endlessly circle of destruction where you all hate each other.

but did something bring you to this point? (or maybe easier: what did bring your relashionship to the point, where your man is not giving you a sence of security and you are not giving him recognation?

- Because he is idiot! (Most of the partners will say about their woman or man), but the truth is that your irresponsibility brought you to this moment! In short, there will not be moment of mutual hatred in the relationship, when both partners can satisfy their own needs, without help of anyone.

I mean, as a man, if I couldn't recognize myself, if I couldn't look in the mirror and see how greatfull and powerful I am... how strong, worthy and cool I am, no matter how much my woman talks to me that I am good, I'd still feel like nothing. It's the same the other way around, and from here we come to another form of irresponsibility, which is the following: if I do everything on my own, why do I need a partner? And yes, your partner should meet your needs, but if it happens when you can't and don't know how to do the same with yourself, your relationship is poisoned (same with money).

As for material well-being, it can be said that our needs are to have a full refrigerator with food, to have mone, car and be able to take care of it, regular incomes, have the ability to pay bank loans easily and so on endlessly, but if after someone appears in my life, after starts satisfying all of my needs, how do you think, we could become grateful and satisfyed, or not?

- How many histories have you seen, that ideal man brings money into the house, fills the refrigerator, buys cars for his family members, is ideal for relatives, friends, is too comforting for everyone, but people still tell him, what have you done for us?

- how many people are giving money everyday to beggar, but his life is not changging?

- Or how many women exist in the planet who are an emigrants. they help to everyone, but no ones life is becoming better. No one is grateful! And the question is, where does this come from?

- Basically based on the fact that if I myself do not know how to fill the refrigerator with food, how to take care of my family and stand on my feet, I just expect someone else to do it for me, and when someone else does it, instead of learning to make same results, I learn how to take help from others and accordingly, **I can become so toxic inside, that I think I'm right, while enslaving person and forcing him to solve all my problems...** the same is with jealous person in relationships, that doesn't know how to overcome his doubts, but expects that partner will do everything, to help him, or her to stop being jealous - he is also poor, and as you can see, poor person is poor in any of sphere of life.

- I think it is clear (says the reader)

- **And you will be right, which is why we come to the next main truth: the first part of getting out of poverty is to take responsibility, in absolutely all areas of life, and to do the same for absolutely all of your own needs.**

- The main principle is that no one is obliged to help you! (You need help yourself).

- Taking responsibility and areas of life.
Now let's move on to the following: any person during his growth, develops specific skills, with the help of which he lives later (skills are different in absolutely every field). For example, womanizers are actually people who have well developed the art of seducing women and making them fall in love with themselves. Or another example: let's take manipulator who manages to achieve his goals with the help of hurt. In other words, he wants to extort more money from you, and if doesn't succeed, he gets angry and sulks until you give him this money, because he considers you feel guilty (this is also a skill). Earning money is actually a skill (the more money you earn, the more you have ability to earn and generate), but self-satisfaction is also

a skill and nothing more. which is primarily possessed by highly responsible people.

However, the ways in which person satisfies himself are different and often unwise.

for example:

Photo in preview page shows very simple principle around which our life revolves.

- Depending on our skills, person has a sphere of

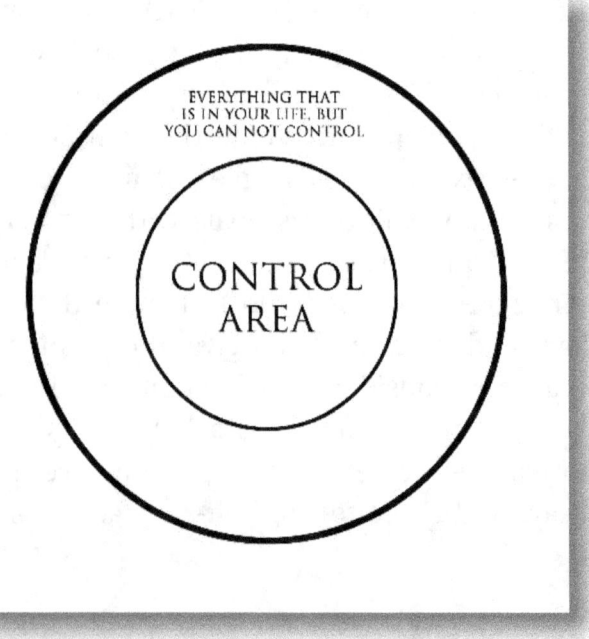

control (that means, what we can manage), but there are many things that do not depend on us, but affect on our life.

Now, just imagine bad and a good sailor. What skills might they have against Storm?

- Basically experienced sailor in his work can in advance understand where the storm will be and create such course in which vessel would avoid this storm. Which means that the good sailor's sphere of control has grown to the point where he can control what was previously uncontrollable, and this is precisely another cause of poverty in any of its forms. **Poor man does not increase his sphere of control, as a result of which everything that we described above happens, and now just imagine how many things do not depend on poors?**

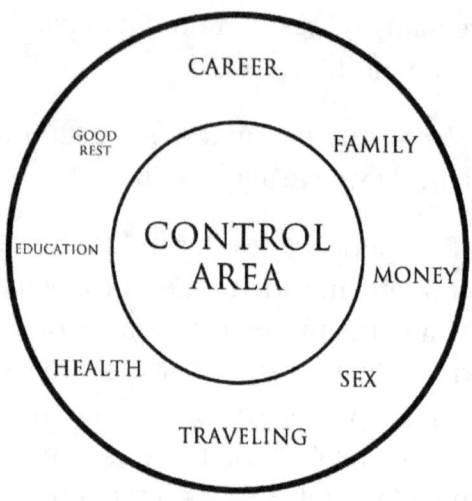

Let's list the main areas of life for most people:

1. For example, take Career (salary increasing do not depends on poor people, because they think that boss should appreciate and notice their work and this is when professional people in their own work take specific courses, read books and study general topics aimed at career advancement which is why poors sphere of control does not increase to the point where career advancement becomes dependent on them.

2. The family (physically ungovernable for the poor and its strength is built solely around the power of the family institution, which is why the poor cannot manage what this institution can no longer interfere with (for example, the fact that women today have much more opportunities and can much more easily Earn more money than standard, stereotypically minded men (which is why the classic roles, where the man was the main character) are mixed up, and as a result, this also does not depend on poors.

3. Finances (represents a brutally unmanageable point in which nothing at all depends on the poor, because unlike any rich person, they do not learn, do not develop. They have not even read 50 such books as you are doing now, in their life, and therefore they know nothing real about money, except that , what the poor taught) - **(but poor cannot teach you how to earn money, because they know how not to earn, lose, spend, give away and not multiply).**

(Think about that: can poor person teach you how to create 7 sources of income? (What I teach people in my Smart Cats book?)...

- of course not.

4. Sexual satisfaction (completely uncontrollable for most people). Let's take as evidence the problem of most men, which is that they can't please women, which stems from the elementary ignorance of what a woman wants, what kind of men women really like, they don't even know that you need to make woman feel special, and you can do this if you blame someone else if she makes a mistake, and even joke that your woman is always right, praise her complexes, because you will be the one who praises what others have cursed for years. Find a quality that no one notices and start praising them. Say that you will be on her side in any situation and over and over again (do anything that makes her feel special) and men don't know it all because they don't grow their sphere of control. They don't study, read, they don't ask anyone else for advice, and so on and on...

(In short, the way out of poverty, as we have already said, is to become self-sufficiency, which is only possible by taking responsibility, which comes from increasing the sphere of control in any area of life).

And this is increased by performing 4 important

actions.

these are:

1. Correct attitude to the problem.

2. Getting out of the comfort zone.

3. Asking the right questions.

4. Increasing the scale of thinking.

Let's take the same situation where we imagine an unsuccessful writer and successful one (I will give you my personal example).

- I know a writer with whom I can say I started my career. He gave his book some silly name, which was difficult, didn't say anything and didn't interest people. When our publisher talled him, that this name will not be good for book, he answer „I want like this and that's it!" (that means, he stayed in his comfort zone), but I... wanted to call my first book „when time comes" – wich was not good for marketing and sellings and because of it, I prefered to call my first book „Dialogue with Death" (I stepped out of my comfort zone and scaled my thinking)). He made a strange incomprehensible, philosophical and high-profile design for his book (when he neither knew photoshop nor had decent taste (that means, he stayed in the comfort zone)), I organized photo session where I knelt in front of the camera and drew death behind me with the help of photoshop. He chose the highest quality paper, with self-lamination, color drawings and so on, which made the book much more expensive to print and therefore the selling price (that means, he also did not increase the scale of thinking and did not see reality). I chose standard black and white paper, so it was cheaper to print and I was able to sell my book cheaper). As a result, two books were released almost at the same time, one of which became the best seller in Georgia for 7 months in a row, while the other one did not even sell 50 copies.

Finally, the author of the unsold book shouted that people don't like to read and don't care about books, so he gave up (that means, instead of asking the right questions, he started blaming others), when the author of Dialogue with Death, by that time I had read about 200 books about marketing and PR (because I was asking myself , how to increase sales), as a result of which I was able to sell my book so massively.

There was one simple difference between me and this author, the things that were not in our area of control, I brought them

under control, but he started complaining and accusing.

- Unity in poverty.

Now let's speak about solidarity, which is actually another major cause of poverty. The fact is that poor people have ideals and behaviors recognized as "righteousness and dignity", which of course stem from illiteracy, inability to control emotions, irrational actions and conformism. Now, I don't want to say that standing by your side and defending your family members, or friends is bad, but when person with all his heart wants for you to live a bad life, **that's a real trouble!**

The fact is that many people on their way to success face situation like: "You won't succeed!", "You can't do it!", "Stop!" and so on.

We encounter this at any moment when we do what no one else does. change profession, drop out of university and start business, Blogging, or choose a specialization that people around us have a bad idea about **and It happens basically because any person on an instinctive level first of all rejects our adventures** (this is normal and don't be worry if people do not believe in you).

But it's also normal that all those people who tell you could not succeseed, actually see themselves next to you when you would not succseed (when you will be in a drama)

 (read from the beginning).

- Ohhohoho! (What we will talk about now are amazing psychological facts).

The point is that for most people the truth is what they have seen, but what they haven't seen, doesn't exist for them, and now just imagine how much prosperity doesn't exist for poors and how strong the reality is that someone doesn't succeed, is unhappy, miserable, pitiful and so on endlessly?

That means, people know how to treat you when you are not successful and happy. they know how to bite you, laugh at you, berate you in a friendly way, or love you when nothing works out for you and you get frustrated, but what if you became successful?

- They can't physically imagine themselves around you, which is why it's very common for a man or woman who achieves real success to find that even their family members run away from your environment. they don't do anything for you to live a successful and good life and also can't become successful with you. **Of course, no one admits that this is so, but is the fact different? (You are alone on the road to success)**

on the way to prosperity, unfortunately, people can see how much their parents and most near people are speaking with a beautifull words, but when it comes time that you need e help from them for the better life, they disapear like never were living with you. But, if you need help in the bad situations (maybe need some operation and

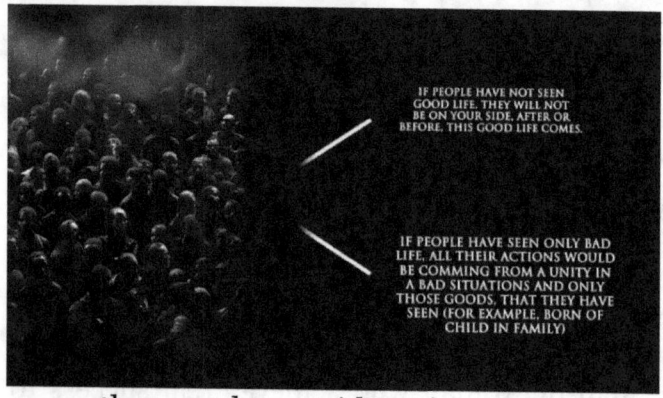

so on, they are always with you).

I know from my personal example, I had one taxi driver as a ,,friends" that was too kind to me and worked for a really cheap price. I was regulary going to him, we always had good ,,hello" to others, but when I bought the car, after two days of it, this man started ignoring me like no one else. and when I told one of my friends, what's wrong with that man, friend answered, maybe you are not telling him hello anymore? (like, I started thinlking about myself that I am too cool now (because I have car), and started forgeting old relatives... after I had created business, because of what most I lost most of my relatives with the same reason and to explain the situation in a simpler language, we will say: **as it was already said, what a person has not seen, does not exists for him, and therefore, he will not be there, because of what, most of people are lost after first success in your life.**

And I understand, it's real trouble. I also understand that everyone says different words and no one ever admits that they don't want you to succeed (they do), but they don't know how, because they haven't seen it and therefore don't exist in the reality where this success is (and if the child is not in trouble, but help , or financing support is needed for a good deed (to buy an apartment, car, get married, or to buy an apartment for child, or to start a new big business, the less these people are in the fine work and not because they cannot, but because they do not see themselves there) and also, if parent along with already talled uneducated, or even manipulative, then things start happening that you can't even wish to your enemy...

The child starts living well, parent scolds him, asks: how can you be happy at this time, how can you be happy, unite, relax and enjoy life when so much trouble is happening around? I will tell you more, very often relatives (not only parents), those who do not contribute to your success, start accusing you, shaming, gossiping and other such dirty actions, which are directly aimed at making you loser and then when their goal is fulfilled, then start loving you.

It's hard to see if you haven't been on this road by yourself (because one side (the one who stands by you in times of trouble) is always right with himself, because standing by you in times of trouble is precisely his most valued act (such people most of all are speaking how a good friend should act and first of all there is talled, that a real friend should help you in a worsiest situations **(and it is really good, but there is nothing spokenn about, that most of such people are living in a worsiest situations day by day and are doing nothing to change there life),** - I mean there value ,,that real friend should help you in trouble" most of all is the manipulation to use others to help you day by day, not the value that helps someone overcome poor life and this people do even for a second admit what you read above, but the other side can't Sometimes achieve so much success to fall into such a reality (to see, ho no one is standing by your side, when you logicaly think, it is normal and good))...

In principle, this is exactly the reason why the majority of people who stand on their feet in one way or another, feel how people around them try to drag them into the mud, and this is exactly what proves the situation, why more open-minded people can see success and potential in other people too (they have already seen success in the life).

Also poor have, such an attitude towards reality that they believe in that these values are valid together and that is how person should live.

It all comes down from five important factors.

1. The norm of life.

2. What is difficult to achieve should be devalued.

3. Having psychological rights.

4. beliefs that reinforce it all.

5. and genetic factors.

Let's start with the first one:

Our brain always gravitates toward what is normal for it, and if poverty is normal, brain will do whatever it takes to stay poor. It is precisely because of this that a once-rich person, who later became poor, will definitely find a way to become rich again (because he has a different norm than those who would have remained in this poverty).

To make my words easier to understand, let's cite the following examples:

1. if parent raises children by believing in their own uniqueness, praise her/him every day, tells that he/she is a genius, cool, special. If parents are too frienldy to each other and are not criticizing, hating and making battles with each other, After growing up, no matter how many times child falls into situation where someone is trying to oppress and convince that they are not worthy, or smart, or are stupid and so on, child will inavitably get out of this situation and will not get used to oppressions **(because the**

norm of life is different). – that means, no one was teaching them to live in a bad life, no one gave example, how mother was used to look fathers bad behavior, or the same from other side, But, if you have lived in a norm, where mother and father hate each other,Where the child is always criticized, shamed, humiliated **(This is exactly what in future people around will do with you and this is exactly what you will adapt to).**

And if you look carefully, most of people unconsciously live in the fate of their parents. (I mean, they are mirroring the life, that they have got used to).

2. A girl who saw that her grandmother was being beaten by grandfather and her grandmother tolerated it. After her mother was beaten by father and first was patient, she will find such man herself and will do everything to live in such reality, because for her it is normal (and normal does not means good)

(how many examples does the world know that the same thing happened in the second relationship, third and so on? (too many and everything is because, victim does not knows how not to be a victim).

3. now imagine Poor person, who saw that everyone around him are poor, if he wants to succeed, he will do everything to avoid success (for example, will start business in a niche and create a product that no one wants. For example, because of good luck this person comes to a strong country from his small one, where hundreds of millions of people live, where any product will find many buyers, but this man will inavitaably start to think and dream about doing business in his own small country), basically because the brain tries to live according to its norm.

Therefore, what is normal is reality.

Therefore, the brain will always begin to strive for this norm.

Let's add to already talled, another psychological fact that people have, and this is the following: ***what is difficult to achieve, the brain tries to devalue it*** (it tries to form an idea, that we does not want the thing, that in reality is too hard to achieve). with the help of which our brain is trying to stay in his normal state.

For example, you have an oportunity to buy a first class ticket on the train, which costs not too much higher than second class

- poor one will say: there are slightly better chairs and nothing more. I can't spend money on this (And then they sit in the second class with thousands of noisy children, instead of sitting in peace, cleanliness, better smells and environment, due to which they could work more easily and better)).

Buy branded clothes?

- The same quality clothes are sold in the markets, why do they need to waste more money on the same quality just because of brand name? (and they go to the market where thousands of people walk. Everyone are fighting with each other, sellers tell you the price of the product based on your appearance, because of what, as pity face you can get, as cheaper product for you is (but what if you are not a person with pity and unhappy face?), Where thievss hunt, often raindrops fall on your head, and instead of entering a brand store and buying the same product with the help of smiling beautiful and sexy consultant who makes you feel like a person, instead of changing clothets in a clean room, were you are safe and secure, and seller does not tells you that you have nothing that they had not seen yet and there is no problem, you can change clothes in front of thousand people, this people will always choose cheaper and the thing that is much more easier to achive.

And this happens to everything that exceeds your norm (both bad and good, the brain says it shouldn't).

- they don't want to become popular (not because they don't want, but because it is too hard).

- they don't want to fight for millions (with the same reason here).

- don't want to become businessman (not because, don't want, but because it is too hard) and so on endesly.

In addition, poor people have too many restrictions on themselves. For them, nothing is possible, appropriate, and dignity lies in adherence to prohibitions. Which does not follow from what is the truth, but

1. from what the rules were in the past...

2. what opportunities does poor people had.

3. in wich moral values they were living.

For example, - who had the least rights in life?

(poor people and slaves!) and if you look carefully, it is easy to see that the children of a successful and powerful countries, that were invaders, invastigators, nor victims, for some reason, allow themselves a lot and people inside are living much more freely (even in sex, they have less taboos), but the countries that have been conquered too much time, people who are living in a poor places on the contrary: are giving themselves less Rights, and it's not only because they don't have money to have intresting life and so on...Most of all, the reason of minimum amount of psychological rights, is that human brain adapts to the life norms, in wich it is trying to help us survive, with a minimum hearbreaking and problems.

I mean, if you something that is prohibitted by everyone (even if you are right and doing the normal thing), your reputation can be destoyed, because of what you will become victim of lynching.

1. For example, it's normal to be protected by the law, yes?

But the poor most of all have the least confidence in the judiciary...

This happens due to elementary historical facts, where poor had nothing to protect, which is why there was no need for a court and also no one asked anything to them. And the rich man had so much that didn't even need this court, because he was able to protect his own values by himself (he would bribe someone, give orders and so on endlessly) and finally the fact was formed that, who have something to lose, but not so much power to protect it by itself, that are middle-class people, where needed in the help of law, which you will see even in reality, in which: among the poor, it is accepted to curse those who go to the police (they are trying to solve problems by other instruments (the reason here also can be that poor has no money to hire normal lawyer), while the middle class are actind different.

I can remember from childhood, how everyone hated the people, who were going to police for help and for example, if your business was victim of mafia, who were coming to you and after taking % from your business (wich you could not denie, because mafia would kill your family members, you, or even everyone you love) and because of what you started working with a police, your reputation was destroyed and everyone started hating you.

And if modern people say (and what?), because today reputational battles are not so scary, in the past, in my country, you life was depended what people will think and say about you and believe me, no one could survive in the world, full of hate and oppressions.

2. also very important is, in wich moral values people are living. **I mean, that in every place of the earth people have diferent ,,what is true" values** and if somewhere by historical facts, unfortunatelly won Moral value, that were created by idiots, after, because of it, people are becoming the victim of their own values.

For example, in the tv series «Слово Пацана», or in English (The boy's word) – if I translated it correctly, there is a good example, of in wich moral Values where living young gang members (in 1980-s), that where after evalutated as a Russian Mafia, that were terorizing people in all over the world.

One of thousands of idiotic values inside, was that gang members need to have an ideal reputation, that can be destroyed by thousand of idiotic situations. Because of what, gang member was forbiden to say word ,,sorry" to someone and if he does it, his reputation was destroyed and person was becoming someone like ,,broken one". after no one gives him a hand-shake, just because reputation would be destroyed too and even your own gang members, who did not defend you from saying this word (maybe because you was kidnapped and tortuned) start hating and opressing you, because of this fact.

To see this situation, in one series the main character, his young brother and another gang member were ambushed by other gang members and after fight, in wich more then 30 boys where against 3 of youngs, the leader of enemy gang demanded from main character to say ,,sorry", that was not accepted by our hero, but enemy took his younger brother, took knife and started cutting the ear, because of what, young whas shouting and adult brother (that was leader of the gang), with fool face of blood, broken nose and bones, said the word ,,sorry", after what leader of enemy gang, said something like ,,you are now the broken one" and with his members, got our from its place.

The idea here is, that broken one, after could not be the leader, or even member of gang, just because of word SORRY?! (that was said to save the member of the gang?)... because of what this leader, brother and the third one are trying to hide this fact and now just imagine:

Logically in any war, in all over the world it is normal to say anything, if you can save your family, friends and people, right? (it is even smart action!) And after do what is needed to do (because lie is an

part of art of war) but in reality, there are too many moral values, that could be built around the idiotic norms, because of what, people are coming the victims, of their own values, that in reality where created to save them.

(In short, I want to say that since the beginning of time, due to specific historical facts, the poor have been prohibited from many actions, by many reasons, started from Moral, nature, or even Physycal rules, but today we live in a different reality, we are much more free, we can manage our own lives (even can read any book we want to become stronger, and smarter) - but these psychological prohibitions still sit in our mind and where the rich will tell himself that he can increase the price of product for example, that is created by him, the poor in the same situation will say to himself, that he has not right to increase the price of product (maybe bread), because too much people are living in a problems and they have no money.

Here I will give my personal example:

- I will speak with my country money value, that is called LARI (1 Lari is now ~2.55 Dollars) and 1 lari is 100 TeTri (like Cent).

For very long time, I had minimal profit from my books (it was not even 50 centes from one (60 tetri to be honest)), which is very little, believe me. Shops, printing houses, partners, advertisements and so on took a normal share, so I was left with less, which means that you will not grow, nor will become rich and it turns out that you could not stand on your feet with this work. Let's add the fact that my books were pirated, some markets where liyeng for several thousand dollars, and in short, everything got me to the point that I am the most best-selling author in my country but have not even 50$ in pocket.

Consequently, it happened many times that I had no more money for printing, nor the strength, motivation, or desire, and in short more than once I had to stop printing books (that means - business died!). once It was necessary to increase the price of book in order to save business, but at that time thoughts were running through my head that I can't raise it, I have no right for it, people don't have money for food, they are in trouble and in short, I had taken all these misfortunes of humanity on my shoulders, but with these thoughts - I still forced myself And increased the price of the book by 1 GEL (100 TeTri). Out of that 1 GEL, I had about 20 tetris

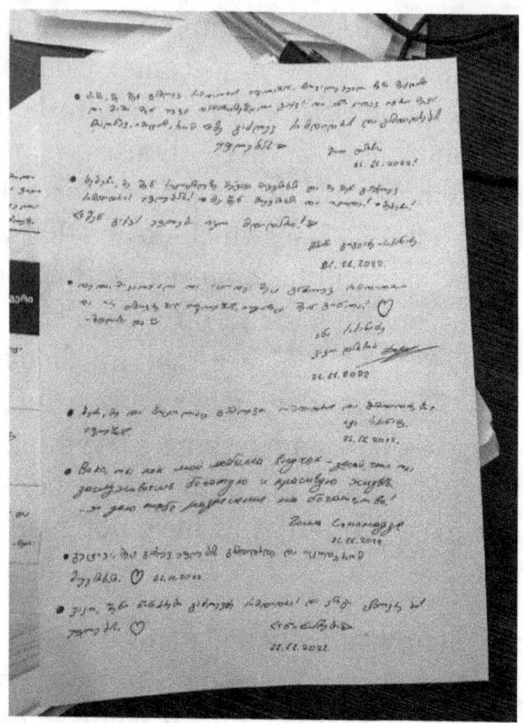

(not even 10 cents) and you should have seen how I was worried and ashamed that I did so bad action, because people have no money for it and instead of prosperity coming to my life, after i always made discounts because of guilty and often sold less than what it was worth before, after which I let my partners lose money also).

Then, once I did a powerful psychological technique related to empowerment, I gave myself the right to well-being by my family members and close relatives (you can see what was written in the photo, but you don't know Georgian and I will translate it for you).

Father: **I am giving you permission to be happy, live in wealth and prosperity.**

Mother: **I love you and I am giving you permission to live in wealth and prosperity.**

Grand mother: same (and same by others too)

Plus, I signed on their behalf, put the date of contract, and on the next day, just imagine, i wake up morning and automatically, start doing new business, after increasing a price to books, consultations, courses and first time in my life, to my mind are not coming thoughts about how everyone are pity and unhappy, that were repeated whole my life by relatives and close friends, but different: I saw a different reality, which was that there are too many people around, who have cars, they can afford to maintain them, they have apartments (when I was a renter all my life), They have families and can spend money together - if they really want something (when in my day no one gives me money), everyone has iPhones and new Samsungs, and they have money to buy what they really want.

It turns out that they have what they want!

After that day, my income increased and I crossed the 50$-s limit for the first time (that is, I already had more than this money in my pocket regularly), then I bought my dream car and in short, a lot of things were changed.

With this example, I want to say that the poor do not even subconsciously give themselves the right for well-bein, and when you do not have this right, you cannot achieve well-being (however, any of your endeavors will be doomed to failure and you will end up in the role of the ideal victim).

This situation will be easily understood by those of my readers who believe that because of so much unhappiness around, you have no right to be happy (which is why, of course, you are unhappy), but the truth is a little different: happiness is contagious, well-being is contagious, and If I had not achieved what I have achieved, you would not have read this book, my dear.

Therefore, those who want to give rights to themselves, take a piece of paper and with the name of the most important relatives, give yourself the rights for prosperity and money.

Sign on their signature and put the date of the contract as well. (you can also write with my name that "I, Vako Darchia, your personal psychologist: am giving you the right for anything you want")

this technique can be used in any life situation. – as much rights you have, much more free you are and better becomes your life.

- Beliefs that reinforce it all.
Now imagine that poor have the norm of poverty, in addition to this, their brains devalue a better life, in addition to this, they do not even allow themselves to live a better life, because of what they carry the troubles of the whole world on their own necks, and from above, they also have the beliefs that are poisoning life and which already on a subconscious level forces them to live in poverty.

I mean, what happens?

- you have no right to a good life, to make new business, become boss, millionaire and so on (because people will say bad about you, or other ,,becauses"), But you have right to suffer and be in trouble, because that makes you human, and as a result your brain, during its growth, looks for and finds evidence that would make such life style worthy and right. as a result, the poor person believes that all the rich are bad, because of what, if the money falls into his hands, he will give it away (to whom is more needy) and in short, they have a whole bunch of beliefs that help them stay in poverty.

I won't say much about all this, because already have said a lot in Dialogue with Death, Man of power and the Psychology of Money online course, but what I will say is this: **to all this must be added no less important genetic programs.**

- Genetically poor people

Everything we talked about above is not invented by one or two people, right?! In fact, everything is much more acute than we imagine, and what if we haave poverty genetically in our blood? What if no matter how hard we try and how much we fight, we still can't escape this genetics?... just as all of us resemble our parents in the way we sit, walk, talk, even at the basic level of appearance, the same is very often the case in psychological behaviors. Even many diseases are inherited by people genetically, and poverty is in a same situation.

In addition to the fact that it is difficult to achieve success when you have to build everything yourself (when it is not about increasing the wealth that your ancestors left, but you have to create it from scratch), even genetically, our body tends towards poverty, and this is the biggest enemy of a person who is on the way to prosperity. Which even stems from the fact that the poor, flesh and blood, have a need to present themselves as ideal victims.

- The perfect victim

Now what we are talking about is very often used in intrigues, political games, businesses and even in everyday relationships, because being a victim is an ideal social tool, which, although will not make you rich, but will save you from cursing, additional humiliation, and also gives you the moral right to make - a kind of crusade atack against the one who treated you badly (or at least you forced him to treat you badly).

There is a famous "Karpman Triangle", the idea of which is that everyone have role-playing games with each other, and in this particular game, they take different roles (mostly unconsciously) - and the roles are as follows:

- Savior - aggressor - victim.

which stems from the fact that people fit these roles in different ways at different times.

For example, you are woman who met a male Gambler whom you want to save (at this point you are the savior), and this man is (the victim). Then, of course, everything doesn't go the way you wanted, the person hasn't changed, he is ungrateful and takes the position of the aggressor, where blames in everything only you and it turns out that you are the victim now. As a result, you need a savior, who can already appear elsewhere, or that man himself can take this role on himself, and so on endlessly.

In short, this game goes on until you won't break the chane of manipulations, work hard on yourself with psychologists, which of course most people never do. **Therefore, the poor are the most vulnerable to victimization.**

No one plays the victim better than them, no one suffers better than them (even if this suffering, is caused by them), because this role, is the best payed by them.

For example, I have humilated and oppressed my old business partner, who falsified my books, but today is playing the role of victim, just to make himself more humanoid and me demonized. Or another example: once I got to the market to distribute books and take money from sold ones. upon arrival, I first time see fake version of my Dialogue with death is lying in one of the markets. (It was easy to distinguish them, just because of quaility).

- I got angry, firsly because did not know how this business is working from inside and it was shock for me, that person with whom I am working, for whom I am making money with my books, just started making money beside my back (with my books)... (and his this action, was marked as disrespect). **Because of what, I started speaking with the older man in an aggressive tone.**

- What is this?! (I asked agressively)

- he firsly started justifying himself.

- and after people started coming around us, he took another possition and tells me that, "If you are a writer, go and write, what do you want here! It's not your business" I told him that I will take this book away now (my voice was shaking with anger) and ordered him not to see the same thing again!

- **STOP!** (you will ask me) Why you just would not go to police? and I will answer, that in our country police is doing nothing with such problems and In many areas of life, we have to live by the laws of the wolfs.

- now let's continue story and thank you very much for interrupting me!

After, I raised voice, grabbed the book, and soon sellers around us gathered (the people passing by were looking at us and this man repeated the words already from afar (when I was going out from this place), "If you are writer, go and write, what is going on here, is not your business" That words drove me crazy and I ran up to him, pulled out his friends and put my fist on his face. don't remember exactly what I said to him, I think threatened, but soon the situation changed and he began to sin. In the end, everything appeared as if I, a two-meter tall man, was oppressing an older peasant man , who didn't do anything wrong, and this man perfectly suited this role (he moved from the aggressor to the victim and brought the people around into the role of savior).

But the point is that actually my aggressiveness was caused by him, yes? (First he cooperated with me, then started selling fake books behind my back (even when he knew me and knew that I am not a boy, who deserves lie), and finally when i put fist on his teeth, because of what he was scared, turned out to be a poor person who was oppressed by a representative of the new generation.

It actually comes down to two important factors:

1. Power games.

2. Unhealthy self-love.

Regarding the first, we will say the following that absolutely all people struggle for power (some consciously, some unconsciously) and **those who do it consciously are well-schooled in**

the fact that people first take the side of pity person.

Because of it any politician, who failed to achieve goals, then takes the position of a victim, where he has done nothing wrong, he is an angel, he is kind, and in the end makes people feel so sorry that he remains saved from massive hatred. All of this comes from the fact that no one wants to be insulted, and the ideal tool for self defending is to make yourself victim, because people will always take side with the one who plays the victim best.

As for the second option, the situation is even worse.

Absolutely every person in the process of growing up learns how to love himself (these ways, not only actions, are repeated at the level of feelings)... For example, there are heavy feelings and These are: envy, guilt, anger, resentment, sin, bitterness, hatred and others.

A person who carries all this in himself is a person who is already looking for the proof of all them outside (that means, what is inside you, you look for the truth and notice it outside). For example, if you have a lot of resentment and anger towards your parents, whether you like it or not, you mostly notice and collect the reasons for the strengthening of this resentment and anger, which is why many children fall into such a big ignorance that they forget all the good things their parents did and remember only the bad and precisely The same is true about sin.

when you feel sorry for yourself, you subconsciously want others to feel sorry for you and the best tool to help you achive this goal, is to become victim!

Sin is actually a form of love.

And the sin against yourself is experienced mostly by the poor people, who themself causes sin from others.

Where now the truth: do you know? I'm unhappy because I manipulated friends and people around me for years, which is why everyone turned their backs on me and today no one wants to make friendship with me...

Or : "I did so much good and how did it turn around... everyone are ungratefull"

Where: year after year, I made my husband feel guilty, which then caused aggression in him (because guilt causes aggression in everyone), which is why he left me! And where: he was traitor and that's why he went to that busty lover.

Where: I am not good in Building relationships with men, because of what all my attention will be focused on my son. I will teach him how to be dependend on me, if necessary I'll put him in shame and guilty, just to make him do everything I want and if he brings a wife, I'll make him put me in first place and follow my whims! And after he starts hating me, because I am bad mother, I will tell everyone: I did everything I could for my boy, but he is ungratefull and he turned his back on me in my old age!

In the end, it all boils down to the fact that the victim: is perfect tool to justify one's own misfortune, which in itself any one of poor people uses.

- Authorities of the poor.

1. Unlike any animal, human being is the only one who depends on his parents for a very long time. Unlike others, we cannot hunt in the first 1 year after birth. Some people are not able to take care of themselves even at the age of 40, and one of the manifestations of this attitude is idealization and overestimation of the situation with emotions.

(In psychology, this is called "naive perspective").

- So? (Reader would ask).

- that means, Children, like adults, have a natural need for security, but unlike an adult, their security feeling depends on someone else, and therefore they overestimate everything, and in their eyes, father is much more stronger and more dangerous than he really is. And mother is more beautiful, relatives are more powerful, specific religions seem more real to the child than they might be, and the same happens in everything that is around child (be it a street, or constitutional mentality) and so on endlessly. **This happens primarily due to the fact that the stronger our family members seem to us, the more peace is inside us.**

(one is if you think that your father will hit someone and make him fly to America, and another that he can't even win in a battle with the neighbor Vanya). Therefore, in childhood, we develop respect for specific authorities and their words (we are talking about the authorities that surrounded us).

- Precisely because of this we perceived failure in exams as a death, and breaking up with the first love as the greatest misfortune.

Briefly, to explain, this is why the terrorist believes to person who prepared him to kill the Jews more than Jew, who will tell him that „I do not deserve to die, because I am a simple person, as you" and this is why, for poor will not ever admire the words of Bill Gates, Steve jobs and other billionaires, or millionaires (Authorities for every one are diverce).

2. Let us add to this fact that any person, or sect that loves and fights for power, first of all, forbids to us everything that is going against their own authority (teacher forbids to raise our voice, parent forbids to go against their word, director forbids to show any kind of free will at all. Any religion - to ask questions. Mafia Laws to raise a hand on (hit) a thief in law and so on endlesly. **(that means, any authority in any ages forces us to recognize them as 100% truth and forbids us to go against them in any way) – what is giving the best results with children.**

3. As a result, person gets to the point where there are too many "truths" around him, against which he is forbidden to move, and here people are already divided into two parts.

First: person who can go against the authorities and

Second: person who is obedient to them.

As for the first case, this is the most important part of becoming adult (even the puberty period - psychologically means going against the authorities. when the authority for the child is no longer mom and dad, but other values (street, friends, recognition, appreciation, fun, sex and others), sometimes good - sometimes even bad values. But in any case, precisely at this time person learns how to go against authorities, as a result of which in the future an individual person grows, who after can have his own opinion, who cannot be controlled easily, and such people can see where they are filled with idiocy, or smart ideas.

but in the second case, when person did not learn how to go against the authorities which for example resulted from a low level of courage, less intelligence, wisdom, many fears, or overly supportive parents, Or with an environment that did not allow them to raise their voice - **that's exactly what the poor means.**

When you can't speak agains your mother when she mistreats your wife, you can't voice specific ideas to your boss at work, ask for a promotion, or even put him in his place when he dares you too much.

When your father treats you like nothing, because you could not defend yourself from him and you hide that you are smoking tobacco - you won't be able to raise your voice in other necessary situations.

When you were taught to respect elders when you were a child, and even today when you grow up, you talk to everyone as maximum polite, as you could, don't be offended if they treat you like a little girl or a boy (which happens to a lot of young adults, sorry for the taftology).

- By the way, the name and the cover of my second book were created firsly to go against people's opinion (that was authority for me), because at that moment, I was most afraid of their

opinion.

Can you imagine what kind of criticism was surrounding this action? and do you also understand that after it I no longer have any fear of people's opinion or their authorities?...

If you carefully look on one very strong reason why people love my online courses, it is that I teach them to protect themselves and even to oppress the oppressor, and this is when psychological authority, ``ethics'', in most cases, teaches and "makes us" that we should not harm others with our work (if the oppressor is evil, we should not teach custumer how to oppress him), but when a person came to me who was blackmailed by her ex-husband, thatwas telling her, that naked photos will be spread on the internet, because of what, he tried to take away house and children and I saw that she was frustrated with going to other psychologists, because they only taught how to look into herself, wich was not solving problem that existed now, I went against authority, with the help of which, prepared beautiful and necessary answers, threats, gave advices where she need to go, as a result of which today that man is oppressed.

In short, I want to give you a task, which is as follows:

Look at any successful, powerful, recognized person (whether they are influencers, businessmen, politicians) and you will see how easily they go against the authorities, while other, traditional life-dwellers, never dare to do so.

- However, with these words, I want you to avoid future wrong steps.

Life can be divided into three stages.

- Traditional.

- Against me/against everyone.

- The Hero's Way.

The first of these are precisely the poor (those who cannot go against the authority), and the second: are already such stupid people who can, but they do not have enough wisdom and knowledge, where not to raise their voice, where not to speak, where to stop and where act contrary.

These are big children (even at the age of 50) who have not understood how the world lives and world lives in such a way that

1. If you destroy your reputation, life becomes hell

2. smart person makes friends, not enemies.

- This is exactly why the second path is called: against me/against everyone. These are mostly the loudest activists, publicly cursing everyone, scolding, cursing the church and other religions, generally taking such steps that after are making to them enemies. Because of this, no one takes such people seriously, and in the end everyone use them in their own political or everyday intrigues (such people are just a resource for the power gamers).

And the third path, ``the life of a hero", represents a person who has enough wisdom to see the truth even in the authorities, to show prudence in going against them and everywhere, always to look for weak points, with the help of which hero does not hurt himself/ goal/mission, but will strengthen it.

- because what?

- you can not become successful if you are making only enemies and also, there are too many ways, in wich you can use the truth, but to make enemies by the truth, is the worsiest way.

1. Another feature of psychology of poverty is scarcity in absolutely everything.

(Deficiency in education (or in skills to use it), scope of thinking, rights, sources of income, occupancy of the refrigerator, desire for economy of money and many others). **– even their debts are too small.**

I know, the vast majority will say that a thrifty person is thrifty because life has put him in a bad situation, and if you give them money, they will spend it as well as nothing, but!

It's one thing: to be thrifty because of specific goals that will take you to a higher level, (increase your sources of income, create assets, and in short use the power of thrift to get your own well-being), but the second is to be thrifty because of fear being hungry until tommorow, if it is alrady continuing for your whole life. and all this because you love a stable income, do not have big goals and are not chasing better life and was inadequaite for a past life.

upper I already mentioned the words: Give them money and see how well they will spend it, because this spending itself, as well as economy, will be aimed at returning person to the specific numbers that he is used to have and in which he lives comfortably.

In short, if you give millions to poor person who lives frugally (chasing discounts and freebies), those millions, unlike a representative of the middle and upper class, will be gave away, lost, gambled, and poor man will buy a very large amount of passives and will end up in exactly the same situation he was in before.

(I mean in scarcity).

And as for the main topic, we must say the following truth: **lot of material wealth surrounds person living in prosperity, not just because he has a lot of money, but because of what he has inside.** What he, she believes, believes, what sees and creates, and where the poor believe that there is little amount of money in the world, that if one becomes rich, other will surely become poor and the rest: person in prosperity believes in abundance.

They believe, that everything in the world is in abundance. There are many planets, and opportunities, and therefore, a person is able to adapt to reality, with the help of which he gets well-being, which then derives from material values.

For example, I didn't buy my dream car because I was lucky, but because through a lot of hard work and smart moves, I created sources of income such as:

1. Dialogue with death.

2. Man of Power (in English-Georgian language).

3. Angel boy

4. Madhouse.

5. Then smart cats.

6. after this book will be also published.

7. Then dirty people.

8. I am also selling self-confidence course.

9. Consultations (rarely).

10. Emotion management course.

11. PR and marketing course.

12. Relationship training.

13. I have my own book publishing house

14. I am going to start other businesses and you can see how many ways I can make money. Let's add to this the ways that I don't use, but will use if necessary:

15. Advertisements on my social pages.

16. partnership way of making money (where you refer people to a specific person and they give you share after seling (for example, I am not a psychologist for children and who is interested, I would refer them to someone else).

17. I will hire a psychologist who will serve those who cannot afford to come to me at my prices, and as a result, customers who can afford 20-30$ will not be lost.

18. Dream businesses, etc...

Let's add to this that any product has its own rates, which in itself increases the income separately. **This is even when a poor person has at most 1 source of income and that too not a good one.** and God forbid - if this one income is help from the government.

How to find sources of good income, I already talk about it in my smart cats, but here we will say the important fact that concerns scarcity and abundance.

First: a person who lives in poverty does not work to develop the necessary skills.

Second: the one who thinks in abundance, on the contrary - works.

- what does this mean? (you will ask me)

- And I will answer you too.

In order to me to create so many sources of income, it was necessary to develop specific skills in myself.

For example, does writing/publishing/bestselling so many books require any specific knowledge? (which only comes with study and practice).

- of course, yes.

- then again: do I was made to make skill of finishing any job I start? (Because there are so many writers who will write a book - pull it up. Write and postpone (never publish). They will write - publish - but will not advertise, because they do not believe in advertising.

- of course, yes.

Do I need specific skills to write with a easy language? (For example, in order to write in simple language, I use the techniques of Stoicism rhetoric, which I had to learn myself) - In order to distribute the book, did I need marketing and PR skills? And then the ability to create courses?

- Good computer knowledge.

- Ability to work on foreign websites?

- The ability to adapt to the new? (For example, last month, my most powerful advertising tool was broken and my income dropped by about 85%) - I had to adapt to situation and develop a new, foreign to me: ability to perform actions, with the help of which I almost returned to my previous income.

- Ability to accept criticism? (When the whole of Georgia cursed my work because of grammatical problems (will be repeated in English, because I myself am translating and editing my books, just to learn English better and after start living in America) - should I accept it and instead of cursing people, should work with the editor in future books?).

- of course, yes.

And these skills my dear, I developed on purpose (some forced, depending on the situation) and that's what any successful person does. But **unsuccessful, on the contrary: does not develop, does not learn, does not adapt, and why?**

- Love for simplicity.
Because they love simplicity.

Another great cause of poverty is living in illusions. When a person is so inadequate that believes in unreal values, because life is so difficult that escaping into beautiful illusions takes away too much weight.

what does this mean?

- that the majority will never take care of their health and will rely on doctors, who in most cases would not even be necessary if person took care of themselves.

- that most people will never read 500 books about financial education.

- will never take courses that teach development

in his field.

- will never use the knowledge given by successful people in his business.

- will never go against the authorities and so on.

All this happens not because a person is just lazy or a coward, but because of many external factors and also as a result of not being able to manage emotions.

I will now copy one of the chapters from Smart Cats, change it a little and you will see what I mean.

➤ about motivation
There is no unmotivated person.

The human brain was not created for a comfortable life, and despite the fact that today we live in the most comfortable period in the history of mankind, the brain itself is as developed as it was, for example, in the „Stone Age". In short, people does not change, or if does at such a slow pace that it becomes almost impossible to notice it, and with these words, I want to say that a person created for discomfort - physically cannot be unmotivated.

- Motivation is an attempt to escape from

discomfort, which means that any person who strives for comfort is motivated, and this is where the most interesting things begins.

- There is no person who is completely satisfied with his life (their brain is not designed to feel satisfied).

I'll tell you more: whatever thing you buy, whether it's your dream house, car, watch, business, whatever: your brain will inevitably depreciate that thing and replace it with a new one after a while, because in the old days, when our enemy was any wild animal, If we were living day by day in the euphoria of how good life is (for example, because we found a new cave), the brain would not be able to protect us from the dangers that might occur.

- Because a happy person is relaxed person and that's exactly why happiness is always temporary! (Your brain does not and cannot release happiness hormone

continuously).

- The brain will inevitably put you into anxiety, nervousness, or fight mode so that you don't suddenly miss the moment when the enemy attacks and I understand that today people are no longer threatened by a tiger running into their home, or an attack by monkeys, or fight to the death with an elephant, but The brain does not understands this. It is not yet developed to survive in today's reality, where there are already different rules, and it turns out that when it forces us not to be satisfyed to what we have - it is both good and bad.

1. It is good in that **every person, for most of his life, experiences a feeling of discomfort that he naturally wants to escape. this is motivation** (that means, everyone is motivated and so are you) and

2. The bad thing here is that we are faced with the choice of where to use motivation (exercise for example, or watching porn?) (and this is used by businesses, states, big and powerful people who try to get on our feet at our expense, which is why we are used to ,, Porn, terrible food, drink, cigarettes, dirty movies and so on, because the brain always prefers to take the easy way out - to lose the discomfort and if you don't force yourself, it will definitely take the easy way out."

In short, if you look fat and don't like yourself, your constant motivation would be to lose weight. (that means, your brain will think about getting rid of this discomfort for as long as possible) and finally you will be faced with a choice, go and exercise, eat right, hire a trainer, run and find out ways to get rid of fat forever, or just sit down and play computer games that will not give you anything and teach you nothing = (But it will remove you from that great discomfort now and also, you as an alive person, don't have only 1 discomfort in any time... you can together feel discomfort because of hunger, cold weather, small amount of money and so on endlessly, wich means, that inside you always are going too much battles, for what your motivation, first of all will be used.

Here is a simpler example:

Which would rather your brain chose? – looking at this girl's photo or video and enjoy it with pleasure, or go outside and fight for the women attantion you liked on the street, that has no interest in you,

until you are not rich, or even have potential to

be rich... who is already being chased by a very large number of men, and you are not only one... you are one from thousands, wich is not good feeling at all. And what if you also are too shy, have no expierence, or even are not handsome? (Which will the brain choose?)...

And if our readers are still on the pages of this book and haven't run to watch 18+ sites, let's say two things:

First: this is why 68,000,000 people every day are watching porn videos (because the brain prefers the easy way out) and second:

The love of simplicity comes from the fact that illusions help people to escape from a difficult life, and thirdly, because of the enormous number of temptations that our society has created for ourselves.

That means, people will continue being poor, untill they take responsibility to do what is hard, not easy.

- I don't know - I won't try!

1. Another problem of poor people comes from the fact that they wants quick results for the expense of minimal efforts, and everything that does not promise already mentioned quick results, does not deserve attention or effort.

This also comes from the fact that majority of people see "what" and not "how". That means, they see how many cars, houses, businesses, incomes, succeful people have, but do not see how all this was created. **But when someone explains how it was created, they underestimate advices because they arae complicated.** They say, "Your words are bullshit - or start swearing and cursing you" because in their worldview: progress and success are built because of luck from beginning to end. (you will win the lotto, or hit the jackpot, will be gifted by nature and born into rich family (this is more real for them than learning, for example, marketing and increasing income with the help of advertising)). **They don't have the knowledge that income can be increased by developing skills** (which you and I talked about above), and this is precisely one of the reasons why people who are new to their business (especially young people) are generally approached with skepticism and cynicism.

people evaluate the world, as we have already said, based on "what" and not "which and how behaviors", as a result of which they see one or two or three people who do something special in their field (what the poor would think is an idiotic behavior and won't bring quick results, that's why they never try same themselve), as a result of which they give themselves the right for cynicism, criticism and devaluation of others.

Here are some examples:

- 1 -

No writer or psychologist in Georgia uses more advertising than me. This happens not because I'm drowning in money (initially I had ~100$ for advertising first time and nothing more), but because I learned to use marketing correctly, with the help of which my activity reaches more people and customers. (Even the haters used to say about me, that I have a really good marketing team), but I don't have no one and if you don't do a good job, marketing can't help you either. What's important here is that people who don't know marketing (competitors for example) think they have right to criticize me for my ads, which is why one or two people have written: I'm not boosted psychologist! (in simple language: boosted for them, means something bad).. If we turn off our emotions and don't just blame envy for such statements, we will easily come to the conclusion that "I don't know — and don't even try" - principle is repeated here as well. (｡ŏ﹏ŏ) and this is repeated in an elementary way due to the fact that the majority of people competing (in any business) have wrong ideas about advertisements and all of them think that if they invest 100 $ now, they have to withdraw 10,000 in five days, and when they do not succeed , instead of studying - they give up.

And also, they are looking what type of ads are using other people and focusing on hate that comes on its ads, because of what they are afraid to do the same and have the same opinion as already mentioned haters.

Imagine three people in the same profession.

First: is a successful, experienced professional.

- Let's call him Jacob.

Second: beginner living by the principle "I don't know - won't even try", for which first one is authority. (second wants to live and do job like a first one)

- let's do not give this character any name.

The third is also beginner, but ambitious, for which Jacob is also authority.

- Let's call him Teddy.

between these three specialists can always be repeated the same games. The last two always rely on the results of the first, and Tedy will try to succeed, because he is ambitious and fearless, but cannot take the same steps, because he does not have same knowledge and wisdom (therefore, he can even do stupid things). The other (nameless) will not even try, but considers Tedy's attempts to as idiotic. Accordingly, Tedy will be evaluated as a clown. **Then the third will inevitably achieve more success than**

the nameless, because where you don't fight, the one who fights will definitely overtake you, so the nameless will begin to devalue Teddy - basically because they started studying, working, doing things together and both have an example of how professional should behave in his work, and the nameless one saw very well how much mistakes was making Teddy.

But after Teddy gains gains experience and wisdom, he will inavitably begins to do things that are giving best results (which is professionalism in itself). As a result, his success will not be temporary, but permanent, which happened only at the expense of the fact that a person became professional in his work.

Accordingly, Jacob and Tedy are already successful, and the second one loser, but he still considers the third as a clown and but second remained to be loser, because he wanted to be perfect in job, just like Jacob, but does not imagine that the one he adores (I mean Jacob), long time ago, used to be a „clown" and made mistakes, which is why he may remain a pretender and clown to his competitors.

3) With the first and second examples, I want to say that while the poor person does not even try, because in his eyes too many behaviors are

idiotic and it will not bring anything, successful tries and gets results.

I will tell you more!

I'm trying become successful out from my own country, and you know what?

- no one is interested am I the author of three or even 92 bestselling books. No one is interested am I speaker of the International Business Forum or not. In fact, all this matters only to me and to those who are happy about my success. but for the rest: in order to become a professional in their eyes and successful in my work, people need to see my "path to success", which doesn't start with an idea: see how cool I am in the other half of the planet, but with mistakes, conversations, energy, content and everything that is the biggest part of success (which itself: a person has to start from 0).

Therefore, those third and second, even if they start copying the actions that the professional Jacob did, they will not achieve the same success, because success and getting out of poverty - depends on the path we take, which is directly related to making mistakes.

Wich inavitably means, that if you don't know

how to do job perfect, does not mean that you do not need to do job (you always need to keep trying).

I even remember how newly successful people feel when they meet the first wave of praise and love. They have a sense of how good, cool and special they are. They feel that they have an untouchable reputation that they have built by their own wit and uniqueness, but that feeling only exists because the **hate machine has not aimed to them yet!**

- because of it their praise goes from one person to another like wave, but when it happens (when hate machine starts its own job and it's inevitable for people who fights for better life), the majority gives up.

- **With these words, I want to say that another important cause of poverty is clinging to old values.** And in old values very often are: people's opinion, their attitude, what they say, think and spread and as a result, person either does not dare to take new step at all, or when they take a step, after are made to see how unfair people's opinion really is (that their opinion is not even interested in truth) and therefore person is faced with a choice:

1. where he, or she should either stop (and apologize to those who where offended due to his striving for a better life, which his relatives will accept, embrace and forgive (because unity in adversity is their main value)), or

2. lose all those people who do not recognize you in new life and also lose the lifestyle you used to lead.

(In short, there is no such thing as a Mafia member and YouTuber together).

Also, Nice boss - doesn't exists (because soon the status of the boss will be taken away, by stronger one) because the world is tough and if you are raised as a good boy, or girl (if you carry the aforementioned good boy/girl syndrome and start doing business like that (where You have a lot of politeness, tact, consideration, entering the human condition, etc. - then be ready that your employees will make you to work on themselves, but not the other way around).

Another example to prove these words would be following: if you are too polite, raised in a very good family, who has already turned 25, you have a diploma and are starting to move ambitiously and diligently in your work, which is seen by older "veteran" competitors, or teachers who are in your business, you should not approach them with the position of "I am your boy or girl", because this politeness will be the reason why you will not be considered as respectable in many situations.

- The right position here would be not childish, but business politeness, where you perceive a person not as "elder and respected, only because of his age and experience" - but as "equal and respected to the extent that they respect you". .

- Wrong dreams.

One ladie told me the story of her family. Wife&husband had several children at home. All were active, energetic, noisy and woman said that her husband every day was too tired because of work and was repeating one same sentence: I wish I could find quiet place and live there, because you have madhouse here!

- Her husband was put in prison after several month (his dream was achived, woman said heartbroken).

In short, you have to be careful what you dream about, voice, or even spin in your brain, because in the world everything works in a such way that our desires can eventually be turned against us.

Now I will not say whether God fulfills people's wishes or not, but it is fact that what about person think, worrie and dreams for a long time, his actions also revolve around that thoughts.

Above, You read one chapter from Smart Cats, in which we mentioned about motivation, that no one is unmotivated and that motivation is an attempt to escape from discomfort. You also read that escaping from this specific discomfort is already done in diferent ways (harmful: porn, TV series and healthy: exercise, proper nutrition and so on endlessly). What is important here, is how big or small dreams person has, because daily life and motivation can adapt and will adapt to this situation too.

I will now tell you how much I did yesterday:

1. devoted 5 minutes to one affirmation (I am tireless and energetic).

2. 5 minutes to the second affirmation (I am completely healthy).

3. 5 minutes (I take care of myself)

4. practiced for 20 minutes.

5. Yoga 11 minutes.

6. worked on the translation of the dialogue with death for 1 hour.

7. worked on writing this book for about 3 hours.

8. prepared posts and stories in three languages and uploaded them.

9. talked to bankers about getting big loan.

10. send all information bank's were needed.

11. called the accountant who has been trying to contact me for a week and had conversation.

12. started watching cartoons and continued (I watched 7 series in one breath (each was 20 minutes long)).

13. went for a walk, but it was so cold, I was walking with a car.

14. conducted a 1-hour webinar and earned about 2000 GEL (~900$).

15. In the meantime, I downloaded new game (it's called Sifu, and with the help of cheats closed it around 12 o'clock at night).

16. went to sleep and continue everything today.

If you look carefully, you will notice that I manage important, urgent and fun job at the same time.

In fact, it all happens because of the environment I put myself in and the dreams that drive me.

- so? (you will ask me).

- The dreams and goals of any of us eventually adapt to everyday life, and the bigger and more real dreams drive us, the more time will be allocated for their realization.

Before I had these dreams, my daily life consisted of standing in the stock market, watching soap operas, going on dates, movies and soap operas again, endlessly playing games and sometimes even fighting.

In short, until I set the right goals and dreams, my body was wasting time, and when I did, it was already using it.

I'm not going to talk about how to set goals right now (because that's already well covered in Dialogue with Death and my Emotional Training), but will say that as long as person's daily life revolves around wrong goals and minimal dreams, that person will be in poverty, and I'll cite it for easy proof. A perfect example is the following:

- Attitude towards time

Time is the most precious asset in life, which cannot be returned, and its misuse is one of the symptoms of poverty.

And, this misuse includes two opposite styles of living.

Rich - buys others time.

Poor - sells his own.

For example,

1. Imagine specialist who sells consultations (for example, psychologist). Such person ties his well-being to time, which means that he will inevitably hit financial ceiling, beyond which he will not be able to make money, because we only have 24 hours in a day, and if you are not the most expensive specialist in the world, but normal person and live in reality - it turns out that You cannot earn more than a certain amount in your work. If, for example, consultation costs 100$ (1 hour). How much can you do in a day?

10? - Of course not, you might be able to do it for a week or two, but soon you will burn out and other areas of your life will be poisoned. Let's add to this that most psychologists who have customers: manage to conduct 4-6 consultations every day. some can't handle even three, and most of them can't attract customers at all, which is why they can hardly sell 1 every day.

- And if someone says that 100 times 6 every day is quite a large amount (600$), such a person cannot be poor!

Let's add such a truth that good work of any specialist depends on his good being, which if he doesn't have, won't be able to produce results and work will be buried.

In short, if you're tired, family situation is messed up, have debts and you're dealing with a lot of other stressers, you won't be able to be resourceful, as a result your efficiency will be small and your income will fall behind.

That's why it is knowns that proffesion psychologist, is one of the most expensive professions, because the biggest expense of a psychologist are supervisions (which means, help of other specialist (psychologist) to empty the negativity you was collecting inside and ask questions if you have). - Plus you will be taxed by state, other large amount of expenses and so on.

Also, let's add that the opportunity to work effectively throughout life is given very little (we cannot work perfectly every day for 50 years) and after old ages knock to us, our incomes will inevitably fall and it turns out that if person, Who for a while managed to make good money with the help of selling consultations (for example making 600$ every day (wich is real only if you have, normal personal brand and good ads – wich also needs no less work everyday)), will not create such business system that will work without his efforts (incomes will also fall here).

- This means if you don't do such business that you built once and it already brings money without your much intervention.

-3-

It is a well-known fact in psychology that very often the most effective people in their work are not the most experienced, but the beginners. And this happens at the expense of motivation, ambitions, energies, which will inevitably disappear in a constant routine job, which can be brought to you by routine consultations and doing the same thing (accordingly, such person will not be able to withstand the world competition for a long time and his efficiency will fall) - in addition, income.

-4-

Let's add to this that life is not limited only by consultations. If you are self-employed, you are also responsible for attracting customers, sales, marketing, intrigues, family problems, dealing with team members, state taxes, debts, human relations, and finally, there are many factors that are importet. It all makes the source of making money by consultations not very happy. (Especially if you are in a field like psychology, where you fill yourself with people's misfortunes from day to day). so if you work in a country where this work is less appreciated and it is impossible to grow on a big level.

For example, famous psychologist in America can write a book once and have enough income that he will not need to do counseling in his life ever, but in other poor and small countries this is almost impossible.

And if you are not self-employed, but working for someone else, there is no less stress here, which finally proves fact of selling your own time is not very effective (which the vast majority of humanity does).

- person cannot be in 4 jobs and build happy life at the same time. Cannot person even ask for a salary increase every month (when owner of his life can even make 100 new ads, from wich one will 100% will work), as a result, person who sells his time becomes a victim of poverty.

Here I will remember, when I raised the price of consultations and they became 150 GEL (~75$) and I was able to sell 4-5 per day. My wife and I went to one of normal hotels in small town in the west of our country (at this time it was first time we gave ourselves the right to just pay for a hotel and do not go as a guests to our relatives (like everyone taught us)). It had three stars, and was first hotel in our life, but was better than many with fives, which was beautiful as inside and outside, had normal pool, good service, breakfast, gym, spa, tennis court and indoor pool. Staying in the hotel cost 150 GEL for one night, with breakfast included.

(I am shocked now, from the situation, that today, while editing this book again – I realizied, that me and my wife are in the same hotel, again (wich today has 4 stars on his logo)).

I remember when we woke up, went for a walk in the snowy yard, I talled my girl: can you just imagine how better we are living now? - That I can change 24 hours of rest in good hotel just in one hour of my work? And Mery was also very proud of me, she was happy and we were sitting with smily faces in the long and cold chair, making rest of our tired brains... although we have to add the uncalculated and calculated costs of life, road, utilities, business, which exist in all of our lives. Then let's add that person needs are growing parallel to his income (it is normal for people), as a result of which one hour of work in better hotels was no longer enough. For some, I had to work for 2-3 days, and in the end it turned out that no matter how much I worked, I could not get the life where real well-being was...

I could not buy tickets to Maldives, could not buy new car and was driving an old Honda Fit, could not make changes in my life the times that were interested for me... (I mean, my life was norm and situations were not changin in a speed as they are going for a rich people).

And on top of that: I didn't have the opportunity to go on long vacations, or to do what I love (writing books), because that would take up time that I could use in consulting.

(Anyone who has at least once raise of salary, or who at least once managed to get better income, even temporarily, will agree with this situation, and no matter how much people think of you that you are rich and have an enviable life, the fact is that money is never enough).

So, finally, to make my life easier and start

making more money, i had to learn how to make money without having to trade my own time (which I'll explain to you soon).

2. Now imagine person who is not attached to time as the majority of people. What would a portrait of such person look like?

- he, or she maybe has delegated a lot of work.

- their product does not require constant work (consulting, for example, does (you get money in exchange for specific time and labor), but in life we can do other type of busineses, That is, a business that you spent a certain amount of time on built once, and now this business is giving you money back.

Such businesses are called surrogate type of businesses.

This are:

- Courses (you record the lessons once and start selling them).

- Books (write once and sell).

- Any enterprise product that is delegated (for example, hire manufacturer, produce a energy drink, hire distributor, put it in stores) - (i.e.

creating a product can be very difficult for the first time alone, but after you build system all this can be solved with minimal time costs).

- Investments.

- or even the most banal: the business of renting apartments, commercial spaces, and so on.

With all examples, I want to say that any person who wants to get out of poverty should aspire to exactly surrogate type of business, which requires a lot of work and learning at the beginning, but after gives you the right to live freely.

(If you noticed, above, in the scarcity chapter, I have listed my sources of income, most of which are exactly surrogate type of business).

In addition, it is true that creating a surrogate type of business is difficult, and it is difficult due to many factors, for example: it is difficult to build a decent team that will be able to solve the case without you, will not steal or lose money. It is difficult to maintain quality and many other factors, but in any case, here we can remember the words of Rockefeller:

- I would rather earn 1% off a 100 people's efforts than 100% of my own efforts. ...

Therefore, this is exactly the difference between the rich and the poor.

- Lies and Manipulations.
I had custumer who was good in Psychology... young man with lot of anger towards his mother and grandmother. As a result of conversations, I heard what kind of good family child this man was. His home was full of love, support and unity. „In short, I lived in an ideal family - I thought", said the young man to me, but when he

grew saw a completely different picture of what his family was like (I see how manipulative and full of hate where my family members).

- At first I thought I was crazy and it all seemed to me.

- More information, please? (I asked).

- **Well, little by little I remembered how mother beat me for nothing.** I even remember that when I was child, wanted to clean house (hadn't finished doing homework yet) and when mother came from work, she beat me so hard that you can't imagine. She was hitting me more then 5 minutes (Then I remember that my grandmother protected me, but today I see the situation a little differently, and one thing I remember is that grandmother looked at my obvious very strong pains and just told my mother to stop, but she did not stop her (just was looking and telling ,,stop, stop, stop!"). Then we moved to another house, we were already separate family, and I also remember that I am alone at home, I don't know what I was doing (but remember, that it was a simple day) and my mother comes from work and finds reason to beat me (maybe for studying, maybe for another reason), but I remember how loudly I screamed in pain and begged her to stop. Then I remembered the facts of other beatings, but when I grew up a little, my mother did not allow herself to raise hand on me anymore, and the beating ended. - Little by little, I began to believe that this woman lives and exists for me, does everything for me (she would buy me pants, or bring a cola. She caressed me and briefly gave me the real love that mothers should give to their children. But today, as an adult, I can already see that it was all a lie... because every time I would not be „good boy" — that means if I was not the boy that is always doing things like mother wants, they shamed and made me to feel guilty.

- Mother and who else?

- Mother and grandmother. Second one was always on firsts side, justifying her, entering into her situation, telling me that my mother is doing everything good for me, that I should not hurt her heart, that I should appreciate her, that she deserves to be loved, that I should be grateful.

So, I always thought that I am an ungrateful and bad child.

- aham...

- Then I noticed how mother hates father (this happened after my parents break up and mother emigrated to other country... she everyday was calling me and asking „how this idiot is living, how this dic*head is doing and so on endleslly (but in reality, father was not bad guy... was not bad father, or even husbend... mother break up with him In a situation when father was robbed by someone and had big financial problems)).

Then when she gives me money and helps me (I lived at her expense), she always has specific conditions about how I should use this money, and if I ask for a little more, she tells me why I couldn't get rid of her - „why you couldn't just get rid of me - why you couldn't get rid of me - why you couldn't get rid of me" (and like that in every daily conversations)... If I ever started a job she was laughing at me, "You and job?! It's not serious", then I also started business with her support, wich later needed money and did not give it to me and finally that I came to the conclusion that it seems that the mother is doing everything to make me dependent on her. I will start work – she laughs at me. will start new business, we will discuss that "we both know and admit that the first investment will not be profitable and it will take more work and need more money to invest (in wich she was telling that will always be with me and helps if something" and when this moment comes, I was always alone again. In the end I came to two beliefs that

1. This person does not love me and wants to get rid of me

2. If she can't get rid of me, then I have to be depended on her.

First of all, two stories got remmebered in my brain.

1. When she found out she was pregnant with me, went to ride the horse to get rid of me (which she said herself).

(if someone don't knows, One of the methods of abortion at that time was riding a horse).

2. Those childhood "sufferings" (for example, when I was baby, I cried and mother put scotch tape on my mouth to make me be silent, because of what I almost drowned).

3. And finally at some point (when I was 25 years old and created family, I said to my wife, that today I am living at the expense of my mother and I don't want to continue it... because of what, I want to say „no" to her money and start making by myself... in wich my wife agreed and talled,

that I can be free and don't worry because of financial problems. We both can even eat just bread if there will be need to survive and she is not with me, because of money and will not have big requests from me). After, I refused her money (told her that I will be able to take care of myself and my wife) and she was also happy, ,,I'm proud of you" – she said, but not a day goes by and this person obviously becomes so abnormally demanding towards me that I get aggressive and start fighting with her... and also asking a question ,,what do you want from me?".

- What do you mean by requests?

- calling hundreds times a day, asking every seco (elementary because I am already man and have no interest to call mother 500 times every day), all our conversations were full of hate. As many times as I called her, she had angry and upset eyes, and all this made me aggressive. I still don't know why I was so angry.

- it was Naturally reaction from you (I answered).

- what do you mean?

- Any person's heart will go to the one who is happy to see us, but when someone meets you with dull and angry eyes, they blame you and start judging you, and this is repeated everyday, will become aggressive and start defending yourself (it's elementary).

- Ah, huh! I also remember how she struggled for our old relationship, where I used to talk to her with sweet words and childish love, and ,,I want your old self" she demanded of me, but how could i give that old myself when I went through hell and had to grow up?

- Hell?

- yes... oppressions at school, outside of school, everyday fightings, discrimination, defamation, in short, I have seen all kinds of filth in my life, and in her eyes I was still the little child who she left before emigrating, or wanted me to be.

- Ah... do you understand that any story has two sides of the coin?

- what do you mean?

- Now you are being 100 percent right and I want you to show me the situations in which your mother was right too (I want situation from here eyes).

- Ah... well... in short, I told her that I will take care of myself and my family, she was also happy and gave me a guarantee that if i need her back, I should know that she alwys is here.

And therefore, when I wanted to increase my education, take some courses, or study, which in itself was worth money and which I could not afford, I went and asked money to mother. But she always was refusing to help. And these two-way signals (that I am yours and helping you, but I'm not!), **it was incomprehensible to me.**

The situation was like that:

- I'm yours and helping you, but let's put Scotch on your face so I don't hear you cry.

- I'm yours, but I'm going to beat you up (and you won't even know why).

- I am yours, I will give you money to start new business and I am here if you need more, but when you need it, I don't give it to you and the business dies, to after make you depended on me again.

Then, a period passes and the relationship between us becomes more strained, we were fighting with each other every day. She was calling to me and telling how bad I am, how I am ungratefull and so on, And once I called to my grandmother and shouted to stop this woman or something bad will happen. Grandmother choosed the side of her child and said, that I need more wisdom and more control of myself... after that, I blocked grandmother and in a few days after one of mother attacks, I went out into the street fully nervousless and crashed my car into a bar, which then cost me big amount of money.

- was something specific that she was repeating for you?

- yes... she was telling me, that I need only money from her and nothing more... and I became aggressive only after period she is not giving money to me...

- was it the truth?

- of course not! I was aggressive because, she was speaking the bad things about my father, because she was attacking me and doinig everything to make me dependent on her. I wanted her to be close, to have delicious food from my mother, to look at me, caress me and hug me. I was hoping that just like my friends can reach out to their parents, so can I. I wanted to just sit at home and gossip with her, but as soon as she separated from my father, left the country, the only thing she gave me was money and nothing else, and after she is telling me, that only thing I want is money?

I wanted her to come to my wedding too, but she did not do that!

- Then?

- Then, let's remember about my wedding, where, as I said, she did not arrive, which drove me crazy. After wedding, she called my wife by the name of one of my ex's whom my wife was jealous of, about which we had separate wars, and my mother was repeating one idea, that: ,,I don't know why this is happening to me" and was leading me to the point that I shouldn't be angry, my wife shouldn't be offended, that we should be patient (grandmother was also in the same position, that my mother is far away, she doesn't know why this is happening to her, but She don't wants to say even a word ,,sorry") and finally it came out that she should not force herself to stop doing this, and we should just get used to a situation, that she is doing it.

Because what? (she is pitiful (like grandmother was telling me)). But you know what? If the same actions were made by mother of my wife, I will tolerate once, second, but the third time I would take my pistol out and shoot her brain out.

And in short, that's how we separated for more then 1 year. where my grandmother was always on her side, pretending that she is sinner and pitiful, and I came out as an aggressor who can't control emotions, screams, and is out of mind (added evidence that at the time, I was on the verge of going crazy and had signs of psychosis (I saw voices and thought everyone around me was traitor), which the family knows and in short it came out that I am crazy and bad, but mother is poor victim...

And that's why I couldn't understand in the end, mother is just manipulator, or I am going crazy?

- That's it!

"Then many more things were revealed about their relationships, and we even saw that his mother has power on "grandmother and other family members". Because of what grand mother is always on her side, not the side of truth, or even friendship and unity.

Also, these stories about psychosis do not come out of the air, and it is quite possible that the biggest reason for psychosis can be a result of two-way signals from the mother. (it is known that one of the causes of psychosis is known to be schizophrenia or schizoaffective disorder, which is also caused by two-way signals from the parents (it is one not only one reason)) and then it was strengthened by the not so healthy life of my client... (so his story is proving itself).

Also, client had good relashionship with his father, with whom they could speak about everything and client asked father „I really need to know, mother loved me or not? Have you noticed something in her actions? (question was created after ideas that were spoken above).

- „she loves you, there is no doubt", but... once we were in minibus. your mother was sitting on a bench, I was looking at her from up and for the first time in my life I saw her merciless face (like something not human and soulless sits inside of her)...

This feeling, like something merciless and soulless is sitting inside of someone – sometimes appears in the victims of Narcisistic people.

At the same time, for the first time I thought about this guy, that he maybe is narcisist, but if it was a narcissist – that means, I was dealing with the most miserable and pitiful narcissist on earth, and after many supervisions, clarifications, searches and works, I and other psychologists came to the conclusion that this person is simply mirroring the behaviors of his mother, because of what I had an idea that he is a narcissist. but in fact, mother can really be!

And yes, I can't have final conclusion, was his mother narcisist, or just unhappy woman who is good in intruigs, but can say the main thing that is intreting for us.

End of story was with a question of this man:

- It turns out that my relationship with mother should be based on manipulations, where I have to play with family members to make them see who is more miserable (to after don't get oppressed by her?), or I have to become her slave and do everything she tells me? or it turns out that I should not continue any of relashionship with her? Just to brake the chain of manipulations?

That's it!

It was a rare occasion when I failed to help a customer win a battle....

if his mother is narcissist, we can't change anything. If we continue to play by her rules, we will find ourselves very unhappy, and the only solution is to break the chain of manipulations,

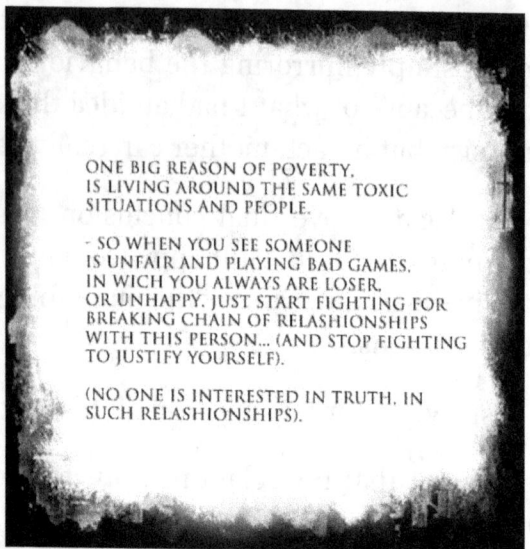

ONE BIG REASON OF POVERTY.
IS LIVING AROUND THE SAME TOXIC
SITUATIONS AND PEOPLE.

- SO WHEN YOU SEE SOMEONE
IS UNFAIR AND PLAYING BAD GAMES.
IN WICH YOU ALWAYS ARE LOSER.
OR UNHAPPY. JUST START FIGHTING FOR
BREAKING CHAIN OF RELASHIONSHIPS
WITH THIS PERSON... (AND STOP FIGHTING
TO JUSTIFY YOURSELF).

(NO ONE IS INTERESTED IN TRUTH. IN
SUCH RELASHIONSHIPS).

because this is where the rules of power come into play, where you should not give the loser a chance to take revenge (which means getting away from her as much as possible).

Finally, with this chapter, I want to say that poverty is characterized by a large number of intrigues (which are no less in wealth too), but the game develops on different levels, and in order to get out of poverty, stop playing in intrigues on the lowest level!

- Exhaustion of resources

If we mentioned narcissus, let's mention one of their features. Narcissists tend to exhaust their victims and then continue living (This is natural for them, and if you look carefully to the victims of narcissist, you will see situation where person will be exhausted because of manipulations and narcisists will give up and leave (I mean, when the narcissist no longer receives the benefits used to receive (money, power and so on), he abandons victim and finds new one).

Almost the same thing happens in poverty. The situation comes to the point where people misallocate resources and each of them leads to ultimate destruction.

- This is repeated in the situation when person buys car to afte rent it and make money, but does not save a penny from the received money for repairs and other unforeseen expenses, due to which car becomes - passive and finally dies.

- is repeated in poor apartment owners who do not take into account the repair costs and consider the full income as their own.

- In a situation where person starts a business, will focus on a specific source of income and will not start looking for a new one until it dies.

Let's take the example of the beginner

influencers who got 1000-2000 followers and start running ads after that. They start Selling any garbage, or even good quality product and they will not start to increase subscribers and do other neccesery jobs, until the resource finally runs out. Or let's take my personal example where I used to run out of resources, which was as follows:

1. First, I had a very big motivational project in Georgia (we had more than 100,000 subscribers (wich is giant number for our country (for you just to know: most popular influencers (who are like Beyonce and Mister Bist in your country, in ours have ~300-500k subscribers)) and I didn't have any other pages or big social networks (except for Tiktok, which I had already grown up and abandoned).

this page after was blocked and I was left without any income as it was my only single point of contact (the business system I was selling from).

Accordingly, I had to learn that any business should have not one point of contact, but others for guarantee.

- For example, China does not buy fuel only from Russia. It has a large package of purchases in Turkmenistan and in other countries as well, with the help of which it does not become dependent on Russia and can force the other side to trade on ideal terms.

- good Construction companies do not have one construction team together. They can also refer others.

- Successful fashion companies do not have only one photographer (they can hire to another).

- And personally, I already have a large number of contact points from which I can reach out to my subscribers and customers.

(This means that I have: 4 Instagram channels (2 in Georgian, two in foreign languages). 2 YouTube channels. 5 Facebook pages (of which 3 are in Georgian, the rest in foreign languages), Tiktok channel, and yes, I have the main point of contact, which is my page at the moment. "Psychologist Vako Darchia" - but if something happens to my main page,crisis will not last long (I will survive) - unlike those who have one point of contact.

- Yes, exhausting the resource does not mean to spoil it by force (for example, if you don't save money for car repair), but it also means the unforeseen factors that

may happen to you (for example, someone take away your house, page, channels, business, etc.).

2. My Second mistake was the belief that I am the best at the psychology of advertising, which was created primarily from the fact that psychological knowledge was added to concrete successes in marketing, as a result of which I found the ideal ways of advertising, where I was able to get very large incomes with minimal costs.

(To understand what I mean, here are the numbers: Dialogue with Death became the best-selling book in Georgia with only $5 ad budget every day).

But the truth is that any marketing trick loses its power over time, and you can't stop at just one ideal advertising idea, because when it loses its power, you want it or not, you will die.

Accordingly, here too I had to defeat the poor thinking that "I found the ideal point and everything will go well" and started to study a large amount of advertising and sales system at the same time.

Is the idea clear? (Any resource can run out, and the poor person sets the moment of this run-out by himself, because he starts moving only after it).

- Perfectionism

In the legends of successful companies, it is often repeated how cool leaders inside were. Even in films and biographical books, the history of how demanding the bosses were towards their employees and how often they set unrealistic goals for them, which were then fulfilled, is mentioned more than thousand times.

- let's take the history of Audi, when its leader made a decision that Audi does not deserve to be in the shadow of BMW and Mercedes and that it is urgent to take steps to strengthen the brand, after which a plan was created with the help of which Audi would overtake these two companies.

In 1979, tests of the newly released Volkswagen Iltis were held in Finland. It was quite an ambitious car, which shocked people with its off-road capabilities. The car was perfect on any road, which the head of Audi used and asked his engineers to do something impossible!

- The idea was to insert the Jeep 4x4 system into a small sedan, which at the time seemed like a nonsense to critics and competitors (exactly because of this, no one took this step of Audi seriously, and engineers were shocked by such difficult task and said that leader is asking the impossible from them, but Soon engeneers came to life and started doing their job).

New car was created, tested, and at the beginning of 1981, was taken to the rally championship, where Audi destroyed absolutely everyone, where 4x4 Audi won the race (now carefully): with a 9-minute victory. That means, Audi reached finish line and after 9 minutes his nearest competitor arrived, which is the most serious result.

And the driver of this car said, "I saw the future!"

1 year later, AUDI Quattro won the World Rally Championship again, and then, to everyone's shock, another championship was won by a female driver, who was said to be lucky, but the women's crew won three times again in 1982 (in Switzerland, Greece and Brazil), because of what no one was speaking about luck of winner women.

- But this is not the end: soon, Audi already took part in American races and announced fight to the legendary cars of that time. It was Ford Mustang, Chevrolet Camaro, Pontiac firebird and others, where, of course, Audi beat them and won the title of champion, after which, at the beginning of the next season, organizers forbade the participation of 4x4 cars, because the big American cars were destroyed by small Audis.

And that's not even close to all the victories that Audi has brought in the history of cars and **Why are we telling this story now?**

Any historic victory, be it in business, sports, or wars, is built from beginning to end on a situation where humanity managed the impossible and created, or did, something that no one had ever done before.

However, today, it is already such an era that seems that everything is alrayd said and done, which is another enemy of the poor people, because as we know, they demand too much from themselves, as a result of which precisely this perfectionism becomes their greatest enemy. They will write a book - then they will withdraw it. will come up with some business idea and say that it has already been done. If they want to become bloggers, but cannot make best content, they start thinking and not doing anything for years, or if they do, they suffer because of the work that has already been released.

Although this perfectionism and striving for the ideal, I know: drives humanity, but let's not forget that there is one thing:

One is, when I'll pay you to work with me and then make you to do your job perfectly, because of what I maybe can be the worsiest boss in the world, but after job is done really good. and second is: that I am demanding from myself the perfect results. (when in reality, I cant do everything well).

Therefore, here is one truth:

In order for perfectionism to be justified (to Steve Jobs had oportunity to produce beautiful and aesthetic products), you first need to have the resources to do it, but if you don't have those resources, you

are doing the job, only in a way you can! (and it is already the victory).

- which is never taken into account by poor obsessed with perfectionism.

I'll tell you more: if you're not ashamed of the first release of your product, that means you released product too late.

- everything or nothing!
You'll probably notice that the whole book has been leading up to this point, as poverty revolves around the belief that it need or everything, or nothing, which itself is part of radical thinking.

In this short chapter, we will discuss the right and wrong approach to risk, starting with a simple question: Have you ever seen successful and rich person who lives by the principle of "or everything or nothing?"

1. with the increase in quality of life, any healthy human, as before, remains focused on the future (earning better life, new material and spiritual sensations). Along with all this, it becomes normal that person forgets his old life with feelings.

(The situation will be easily understood by those who no longer travel by subway (you can't start thinking every day about how good subway was, how smelled inside, and how someone is offended that you no longer ride the subway with them. - a person will simply continue to living and focus on current situations).

2. Therefore, if person is normal, he will never aim to lose everything he has built so far (this action goes against the natural rules) - human goal will at least take into account that if the case does not work, he will not end up in a worse situation, and if the person is wise , will only take up such business, which will not follow his family members behind him (that is, he will not take such risk that is not worth it).

3. Let's add another important fact, where really big money comes only to people who take the most risk on themselves (not exactly normal ones), although this risk should always be taken in the right niche.

- what do you mean? (You will ask me because you are smart and I will tell you).

- In any business, money comes from two important interdependent factors.

1. Scale - that is, how many people and customers your business goes through.

2. margin - how much money you get from each sale.

Both the one and the other are actually measured by reality, and in a poor country (such as Georgia), it is physically impossible for most businesses to go on a large scale an margin.

(To understand what I mean, take the following: imagine that you want to advertise your book on Facebook in America. Accordingly, you will mark (books) in interests. Facebook will at the same time throw you at least 61,000,000 people to whom you can show your ad (that means 61 million people who are interested with reading books)), but in my country (Georgia) we are only 3.5 million people, and imagine how many of them are interested in reading nooks after finishing the school?

(And almost the same thing happens to most businesses).

Therefore, when you can't become rich in scale, you should still take it with profit, because one is to sell 100,000 products with a profit of 1 cent and second is the same number with 10 Dollars. But here too you hit the ceiling of reality, where no matter how much I trust your product, I can't physically pay you a lot of money (for example, you cant sell 100 000 Rols royce in Georgia for real price).

Therefore, a big risk should be taken only in a niche where you will get a suitable reward, which is at the right point between risk and loss, but the majority of those who are in the wrong niche and live by the principle of or everything, or nothing, unfortunately - pursue an illusory reward that you niche cannot offer to you physically...

Therefore, such risk is pointless.

The point is that at low level of life, there are lot of things that won't get you in choise for „everything, or nothing" if you do job smartly, but at high level, when you are fighting for a giant results, money and power, there's high chance that you'll get to exactly nothing. and how do you think why?

You can compare situation to MMORPG game, where your 1 level character can destroy at most 5-10 level enemies, but not 100, and to do it, you must at least assemble very good team, all of you need to be with ideal equipment and higher level. in short, You need to prepare seriously. (only after that it becomes possible to defeat the biggest enemy), but if you don't go through that path and practice on 1-level enemies, then 5, 10-level and so on, you won't find the right friendship, you won't find people with common interests, you won't find equipment, gain experience and eventually lose.

4. In addition, the worst thing that can happen also is to fall into an attitude towards other poor people.

- what does this mean?

- Other traditionally minded people probably already live in "nothing" and in your attempts to get out of it, you will more than once encounter their distrust, rejection, non-acceptance and inability to take risks. You may even need their meager resources to do the job, and if it doesn't succeed, then be ready for the legendary battle against you loved onec (because man is more forgiving of killing his father than loosing his money). But in the end, person who clearly possesses great potential, who is really "better" than others even in terms of having the ability and knowledge to take risks on him/herself, is quite possible to fall into the debt of the weaklings, who are so numerous and so well-versed in uniting against anyone, that Future attempts for figting with poverty, may not be successful.

- They will hinder you, spoil your name, and this new fight (not for your goal, but for survivaing), may kill all your dreams.

5. Add to this the fact that when you start working step by step and really move to a higher level (there you will start earning 100-200-500 or even 1000 $ per day), all those weak people will automatically leave your environment for many reasons (even because , that they did not

see themselves in success and therefore do not exist there), which is why the environment will inevitably change. **People of a completely different level will appear next to you, with whom you talk and work, not gossiping and wasting time, but implementing ideas and improving life.** Then there is an opportunity to attract better investments than those poor people will be able to give (even bank will be ready to give you much more than they can), and accordingly the chance of success increases greatly and the chance of coming to "nothing" decreases.

And what was the reason of it?

- not fighting with a goal „or everything or nothing" but fighiting with a goal „become better step by step".

- What governs our price? (in money).
In material, but not human-moral-ethical norms, all of us receive as much money as we worth.

In general, how kind, beautiful – or bad person you are, does not depend on how much money you make, because there are many evil - poor and rich people, as well as good poor-rich people. However, in the material world, people get exactly what they worth (no matter how sad it is).

And this price is determined by several factors:

1. Where is person located on the world map?

2. What type of skills does person has?

3. How does person occupy a psychological position between consumer and producer.

• Now look, in one of the very cool books (whose name I don't remember), I came across the story of father giving his son watch and telling him to sell it in very expensive price (the book could have been "The Richest Man in Babylon"). Son first went to the "market" and tried to sell the watch there, where people told him that watch is not worth anything and they won't pay much, then he went to another place and the same thing happened there, and finally he came to the person who knows, buys and sells watches. **who offered the young man much more money than his father asked for.**

The lesson from this story is that it really matters a lot where you are located.

And I understand that it is terribly unfair

and sad, but in a successful country, person has much more value than in another. This very often happens that one successful country is built at the expense her victim.

• But are there people in any country who earn much more than others in the same profession (in the same job)?

Of course!

For example, when you have:

1. Self-presentation skills (which can be personal brand building, adaptability, sales and product development skills, or the ability to not make the same mistake hundred times, etc.).

2. ability to take more risks on yourself (of course), no matter in which country you are, if you have more effective skills than competitors, the more your material price will be and more money you will bring to family.

But what is sad here, is that if you are even best specialist in the world, but living in a bad non successful country, worsier competitors in other country can live much more better, then you are doing here (even if you are successful) – because we are paid the money that we worth.

Simple examples of these words would be:

1. poor person, who could not find job in his country and went to another and there too cannot find a job (because he does not have the skills to find job), thinks that problem in reality is in something else, that in his own country are problems with a jobs and also in America are problems with a jobs, but the reality is, that this human – is just payd what he worths, because : just going to a better place, does not means that you are becoming better.

2. Let's take successful bloggers from post-Soviet countries, who, if they succeed in their own language and business, will see that they can't grow any more and it turns out, they should go where is much more potential, but how many people do we know who went from the post-Soviet countries and succeeded in America (by doing the same thing)? (these are units) because

First: your experience can even become big problem in another country (because what you did before may be considered as the actions of dinosaurs elsewhere) and

Second: if you haven't burned the bridges to go back, it turns out that your energy and efforts should be spent simultaneously on working in several languages (that means, (now just imagine), you are an successful YouTuber in small country like Georgia and you are making content for 100 000K sucscribers. ADS – are not giving you lot of money, but you are making some, you have fans that love you and because you could not see real successful future here, you are going to America to become better.

After you want to become Youtuber in English, because there is much more potential and if in Georgian language are speaking only 3.5 million people, in English is speaking half of the world.

So, If you are not burning the bridges, you will be made to make both, Georgian and English content at the same time, right? (and you will tell me that, it is not problem, because you can always hire a translator and so on, but there is problem, that you cant make so much money with this job in your small country, just because, everything costs expensive and your ads are not giving so much money, to delegate everything to everyone and you also, as a child of poor people do not know how to delegate the job)... soooo!

- it will eventually come to the point that you will not have cool content in Georgian, nor in English language, but after you 100% will see that you are more valued here (in Georgia) (because you have invested more energy over the years and also understand the cultural norms) and in order to be able to succeed in English, you need to invest even more energy there, which becomes almost impossible, because

First: for this, you need to transfer 100% focus to a specific task (which means that old tasks should be either ideally delegated or abandoned altogether), but if you had a perfectly delegated and organized life, you would not move to another country and foreign environment in search of a better one, and

Second: you do not have so much energy in elementary way because:

1. you see yourself in a gigantic competition where everyone knows more than you in the aspect of success and

2. The spirit of youthful rebellion that used to drive you before is no longer physically active, Which is why, in the end, even a successful person in a particular country does not manage to achieve the same, or even more, success in another country.

If I were to explain it to you with my example and give you personal advice, then I would say this:

- First of all, take care that you get to the right country and the right environment there, and don't waste a second of your time on anything else, because today my biggest enemy to succeed in America is not the giant competition in which I have to surpass other psychologists and writers, but the competition Between my already accumulated results and dreams I am pursuing. because the accumulated results in Georgia are very much preventing me from entering the American market with all my focus and strength.

Therefore, it is difficult for me to even describe how difficult it is for me to devote time to the dream of translating, publishing, testing, advertising, and content of my own books in English, while here I have thousands of readers and users who need endless attention and care and solving problems. But of course, here is no bigger potential than I already have.

- Fears!

And finally, perhaps the greatest enemy of the poor.

- now look: any emotion and feeling is first of all our best friend and aims to survive/reproduce. If you didn't fear anything, you'd run into fire and get burned, or get into a hand-to-hand fight with bear, after, of course, become murdered, but our brains differ from other animals precisely in that we can judge what is right and wrong. **We can ask questions, think critically, and manage our emotions, or even instincts.**

It is generally known that the brain is divided into three parts.

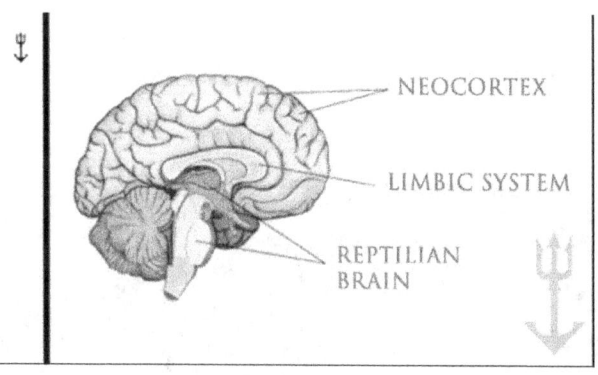

Neocortex is responsible for (thinking and intelligence). The limbic system is about feeling and emotions, and the

reptilian brain is about instincts and survival. However, unfortunately, in the majority of people, these ,,brains" are not very friendly to each other and sometimes appear chaotic (where for example emotional and rational intelligence is not developed, instinct will take responsibility for managing person) and then this person will enter social networks, listen to some video, will not undarstand what is going on her and what about author is speaking, but will start cursing and hating author because of what he even had not said, or mentioned.

In short, successful person is first of all human who has all three ,,brains" developed and well processed , but the one who does not work on himself, as we have already said, becomes victim of the chaotic work of his own brain.

AMOEBA - SIMPLEST ORGANISM

For example: take the amoeba, which is the simplest organism that fights for survival by the "far-near" principle, which means that amoeba will not come close to something that could potentially kill it, but will come close to something which will be good fot it.

his is the main principle of how emotions are working (I mean, our emotions also work according to the far-near principle), which means that we kiss, hug and love good and keep everything bad away.

-no healthy one will starts kissing with the bear, yes? but when person does not work on himself, it is quite possible that instincts, desires, temptations and everything else will win, after which person will approach and start friendship with what can be his greatest enemy. (For example, he will go to the casino and lose house, then start friendship with a manipulative person and so on endlessly).

In short, fears work exactly like this principle.

- I remember situation when, during student

years, I went to visit two young people who lived together and not a long time passed, both of them talk with obvious anxiety about the fact that they do not have money to pay   apartment tax (because the salary was late) and they were afraid that the owner of the house will throw them out. give a notice , or even make some problems (they told me he is a serious man and does not like to wait) in short, after five-minute of conversations, with full confidence I said: that it is normal that sometimes in life things did not go as we wanted and everyone knows about its truth), therefore if you humanly and politely explain to the owner that it is very difficult for you now and you will give him the amount little later, nothing bad will happen... after my words, boys gained courage, called him, explained the situation and Surprise!

Owner answered, that there is no problem and talled them ,,even if you need more time, tell me - the main thing is to warn me in advance - and that's it, okay?". Problem was solved and what these two were afraid of, turned out to be not dangerous at all.

- Now just imagine how many irrational fears drive the poor people, which they either perceive as prudence or some other good values, and you will see why there are so many poor people around.

- Yes, the majority of your poor relatives are simply cowards and not prudent an you my dear, if you are interested in more about business, success and power psychology, just start reading my Smart Cats now.

the end